D1547660

AFRICA
THE FINAL FRONTIER
FOR BUSINESS

INVESTING FOR PROFIT AND IMPACT IN THE
WORLD'S MOST PROMISING MARKET

EVARISTUS NKONGCHU, ESQ.

Alkebulan Ventures, LLC

Acknowledgments

I would like to thank my wonderful wife Maria Nkongchu for all of her relentless support as I've gone through the process of completing this book. Thanks as well to my children for their love and for keeping me grounded. You mean everything to me.

I would also like to thank all those who provided critical insights and feedback during the writing of this book, especially Jerome Ringo, Barrett Raftery, Isabella Erawoc, Tim McCollum, Mouchili Mayoua, and my development editor David Kirshbaum.

This book is dedicated to all who believe in and work for the vision of Africa as a continent of peace and prosperity.

Table of Contents

Introduction

Something big is happening in Africa today, a development so staggering in scope it is restructuring the balance of power and influence in the global economy. Companies that jump on this opportunity can realize massive, sustained growth and lead almost any industry. And if they do it in a way that includes and benefits the people of Africa, they'll be able to continue reaping the rewards for as long as they want.

On the other hand, businesses not operating in Africa are going to find themselves marginalized in the coming decades. As soon as 2025, consumption spending across the continent is projected to reach $2.1 trillion.[1] And with projected rapid population growth and economic expansion, that's just the tip of the iceberg.

You're looking at a market that will change the balance of world power. If you don't find yourself set up within this continent, you're going to be on the losing side of that shift. So for a long time I've been asking myself, where are the US companies? Why don't they see what's going on and how important it is for the future of their business?

The US has been falling behind and missing out on this opportunity, while other countries, China in particular, have made massive gains in terms of influence and market control. Until recently, the US has remained overly focused on military influence and aid, underscored by a political/ethical stance that sometimes worked against the best interest of all. Meanwhile, China and others have taken a purely economic approach, strengthening the position of Chinese-state affiliated companies. Only a few US industries, oil and gas in particular, have invested heavily in African development. We have been missing the bigger business and economic opportunity.

And we have also been missing the opportunity to be the global leader for a just and sustainable approach to economic development in Africa. In my opinion, compared to many other countries, the US has a higher ethical standard, and it has an advantage over Europe because it was not involved in the late 19th century wave of colonization in Africa. However, America has not been fully leveraging the advantage of its reputation.

Fortunately, this has begun to change in the last couple of years. Policy shifts from the federal government have paved the way for increased involvement of US businesses overseas, with a special focus on Africa. In particular, the recent establishment of the US "Prosper Africa" Initiative and the International Development Finance Corporation (DFC) marks a huge turning point in US-Africa relations. In this book, I'll be sharing more about these changes and what they could mean for you. I've been very encouraged to see them, and truly, they make this the best time ever to get in on the action in Africa.

I'll focus on Sub-Saharan Africa (SSA), and I want you to come away from this book understanding the three critical benefits to greater US business involvement throughout the region:

- the benefit for your business and the US economy in general
- the benefit for the people of Africa
- the benefit for the planet (and thus the long-term global economy) in developing Africa in an environmentally sustainable way

I'm going to show you the how and the why behind these benefits. I'll also show you some of the likely consequences of failing to act on this opportunity or of going about it the wrong way.

Who Should Read This Book?

Well, in my humble opinion, everyone in America should read it to gain critical knowledge about the most dynamic and misunderstood continent on the planet.

But in particular, you should read this book if...

- you're looking for hot investment opportunities.
- you want to make money while making a real and positive difference in the world.
- you already have operations in Africa and you're interested in opportunities to expand.
- you've thought about expanding your business into Africa (or overseas generally) but heard it's too hard or risky. Things are changing fast and this book will challenge you to rethink your assumptions.

Several great books and hundreds of articles and papers have appeared in recent years about the rapid economic development of Africa, its business opportunities, and its unique challenges. They often focus on data and statistics—what is visible and quantifiable.

Those metrics are important, but what's not being discussed much in the West is what is hidden from the view of outsiders—for example the vast informal economy, the cultural norms governing how deals are made and relationships formed, and the experience and perspective of Africans themselves.

Yes, I'll present some key facts and figures (drawing on some of those excellent works I just mentioned), but I also want to provide a more personal window into Africa and the relationship that could exist with the US.

So I'm going to be including some personal perspectives and accounts of my experience and knowledge of both SSA and the US. There is too little understanding between them, and I hope to bridge that gap.

There are people who will disagree with me. I welcome that. My goal is to open up a conversation on what I believe is one of the most important topics in our global society—the infrastructural and economic development of Africa.

Who Am I to Write This Book?

Now, before I go further, why have I dared to write such a book? And why should business leaders and investors listen to me? As a licensed US-based attorney born and raised in West Africa, I have a unique perspective that can help both sides benefit. I bring with me the American way of doing business, and above all, the ethics of a US-based attorney. I have the additional advantage of being an African with a unique knowledge of the landscape, the people, the culture, and the customs. I am a student of the continent.

I understand the American business and legal system, and I also understand how things *really* work in Africa. The latter is often not "by the book," but if you know how to operate in a smart way, you can create predictable success. Being African and tied to the culture and history of the continent, I can help you understand how to find the hidden doors and gain access to opportunities that would normally be shut to outsiders. I also maintain a strong network of experts on the ground throughout SSA to advise on local considerations, vet business opportunities and partners, and ensure smooth transactions, so I am continually updated about events and trends in various regions

A few more things to know about me:

- I am a practicing, licensed, US-trained hybrid attorney with over a decade of experience at almost all levels of the US legal system, both state and federal court, including multiple Circuit Courts of Appeals
- I believe the time has come for the people of Africa to gain the benefits of the resources held within their land, and to enjoy economic prosperity and a comfortable, secure quality of life
- I believe US companies have a key role to play in developing Africa humanely and sustainably. And I believe that in doing so, they will **realize high levels of growth and profit while providing global leadership for decades to come**.

I hope by now I've piqued your curiosity. So let's take a slightly deeper look at *why* there is such a huge opportunity in SSA.

The Trifecta of Economic Opportunity in Sub-Saharan Africa

Three converging factors make Africa, which is the birthplace of humanity, also the birthplace of its future.

1. A huge, young, fast-growing population
2. Vast natural resources and undeveloped land
3. Extreme lack of physical and economic infrastructure and business development relative to the rest of the world

Let me give you an overview of each of these factors.

Huge, Young, Fast-Growing Population

You cannot say anything about Africa without starting with the population explosion. Africa is the second-largest continent in the world, and right now, it's the second most populated continent, with over 1.2 billion people. So there's already a huge potential for development.

But more importantly, the population is growing at a much more rapid pace than elsewhere in the world. And unlike many other countries, the younger generation far exceeds the older in size. In Europe, by comparison, the population is skewing older. In Africa you have it the other way around, which means a lot of workforce, a lot of people to feed, and a lot of families creating an even bigger future generation.

According to the United Nations, "More than half of global population growth between now and 2050 is expected to occur in Africa. Africa has the highest rate of population growth among major areas. The population of sub-Saharan Africa is projected to double by 2050."[2]

Of course, projections are subject to many variables, but even more conservative estimates show Africa being the world's dominant population center. Stanford University's Hoover Institution published a comprehensive report in 2019 on population growth titled *Africa 2050: Demographic Truth and Consequences.* Author Jack A. Goldstone wrote that the mid-range projection showed Africa growing from a population of 1.2 billion in 2015 to 2.5 billion by 2050, and then to 4.5 billion by 2100. Percentage-wise, that would mean an increase from 16% of global population to 26% (2050) to 40% (2100). And these increases actually assume a significant *decrease* in fertility rates in sub-Saharan Africa over the same timeframes. If the number of births per capita doesn't decline as much, the population numbers could end up even higher.[3]

Nigeria's population alone is expected to reach 1 billion by 2050, while Africa's total working-age population will grow to a similar size (more than India or China).[4] This rapid population expansion is creating immense challenges and opportunities for planning and developing systems and structures capable of supporting so many people.

The Rise of the African Middle Class (and the Millions Left Out)

Along with this population explosion, a thriving middle class has begun to emerge in Africa. Many are educated in the West. They're young, have money, and are hungry for opportunity as well as for modern comforts and conveniences.

This is a positive development, but it could also lead to new problems. On the one hand, you have a large group of people getting a better standard of living—the educated ones—but it's not happening for everyone. There are millions stuck at the bottom. What's going to happen to them? They're already struggling, and they're falling further behind.

There's economic inequality all over the world, but in the US and other developed countries, at least there's some structure. In Africa, we're heading toward a situation where there's the 1% at the top, a sizable middle class, and then a huge population all the way at the bottom without structures in place to help—no safety net, no hospitals, no access to education, and no support. This is a disaster in the making. If the COVID pandemic has taught us anything, it's how interconnected our world truly is, and therefore it behooves us to look ahead and prevent mass crises wherever they might develop.

This population relies on an informal economic system, and while this informal sector is rapidly being engulfed in a wave of modernization and integrated into formal economic structures, it still drives much what is going on across the continent. The more US companies can guide the transition so it benefits and uplifts people, I believe, the better it will be for both sides.

Vast Natural Resources

Africa has always been known for its natural resources, and for good reason. It's estimated that 30% of the world's resources are in Africa.[5] Precious and semi-precious minerals, energy resources (both green and non), all manner of flora and fauna—whatever you need, it's there.

Also, nearly 50% of the world's uncultivated, arable land is in Africa, according to the Brookings Institution.[6] Now, that should blow your mind. In the entire world, of the land that has not been cultivated and could be, almost *half* is found in Africa. For agriculture, it's the final frontier.

But what's even more mind boggling is that Africans are still importing food—a lot of food ($35 billion-worth in 2017, and estimated at $110 billion by 2025[7]), which further highlights the development opportunity. The resources are there. The demand is there. There just aren't enough people and businesses bridging the gap between the two...at least not yet.

Lack of Development

That's not just a problem in agriculture—most consumables of all kinds in Africa are imported. And this is largely due to the fact that despite the growth of the young middle class and an abundance of land and resources, the sub-Saharan portion of the continent remains largely undeveloped. When I say undeveloped, I mean across the board: electricity infrastructure, roads and railways, financial infrastructure, water and sanitation, health care, manufacturing...you name it.

None of these deficiencies make sense, but that last one, manufacturing, is especially crazy—all those natural resources, and almost all the processing is happening somewhere else. Take, for example, mobile phones—a lot of the raw materials for their production are mined in Africa, so you might expect that manufacturing would also happen there. It's going to be less costly to harvest those resources and not have to transport them somewhere else. And the labor cost in SSA is extremely low.

But right now, African countries are primarily just suppliers. They produce the raw materials, and in a small percentage of cases add some initial processing. There are a number of historical reasons for this situation, but we need to move past them. The time has come for a major change, and it is already underway. It creates an array of opportunities for those willing to think outside the box and recognize that they can do great in business by creating opportunities that uplift people.

If you combine all these factors, what you end up with is a game-changing development in the global economy. I believe it's a huge opportunity specifically for US businesses—an opportunity for massive growth, global leadership, and making a huge difference for millions of Africans the world has thus far left behind. Truly, whoever establishes a dominion in Africa in the coming decades will lead the world.

Overcoming a Dark Past

A lot of the business activity that has taken place across the continent has amounted to a grab by elites and foreigners for resources, power, and money...a grab that leaves the needs of Africans out of the picture, especially the poorest and least educated.

You only have to look at the state of development to see this is the case. How can a continent so rich in every resource be so poor? Africa has everything needed to be the most powerful continent in the world, yet millions of its people have nothing.

Africans see their resources being taken away, with their livelihood destroyed in many cases. They feel unincluded and uncompensated. As the situation becomes more desperate for the have-nots, and frustrations mount, an increase in violent confrontation becomes likely.

Consider the oil pipeline saboteurs in Nigeria. If you've never heard about them, these were poor fishermen whose territory happened to have oil underneath. A deal was struck, but the stakeholders neglected to consider the needs of the people living where they were operating. Their fisheries were polluted and their way of life destroyed.

What would you do?

At the same time, climate change is causing water sources to dry up in this arid region of the world, placing additional pressure on the most vulnerable populations. This is also threatening the small amount of electricity production, much of which relies on hydropower. One approach to dealing with this situation has been to turn gas into electricity or use fuel-burning generators. This is obviously not a great approach, given the rapid onset of climate change, yet renewable energy production is not scaling upward as fast as needed.

It doesn't have to be this way. In this book I'm going to make a case for a new way to do business in Africa.

Recognizing the Opportunities

Africa is the place to start looking at new areas for business growth and innovation—it's about the lowest hanging fruit. Oil and gas is where everybody tends to focus, including US companies. But what about all the other industries? I'm here to tell you there are a ton of other opportunities that are being missed.

Consider mobile phones. Many believed that other developments would have to take place first, but now phones are all over the continent, despite the lack of roads, electricity, and various other forms of infrastructure. That industry is now largely dominated by South African mobile network company MTN and Chinese manufacturer Transsion.

Pioneering companies figured out ways to get into the most remote villages and get phones in everyone's hands. People might not have much food, and their only power might be from a gas generator or a community charging station, but they have mobile phones. And their proliferation has led to other unique developments, like the rise of mobile banking.

Whatever your industry, if you want to compete and stay relevant, you need to be there, because that's the frontier. It's ripe for massive growth both in basic goods and services as well as for innovations that will lead the direction of the global economy for decades to come. The time to get in on the ground floor in every sector is now.

The Cost of Inaction

Truly, the benefits of getting involved in Africa today are huge, but there are other, secondary reasons to get in now as well. We'll explore these in more detail later in the book, but I want to introduce them now.

The Chinese Connection

In recent years, the Chinese government, both directly and through Chinese businesses, has made strong inroads in over 40 African countries. They've been investing in infrastructure projects, natural resources, and many other areas, increasingly even ones where the US has historically been strongest, like venture capital, private equity, and foreign direct investment.[8]

This has some benefit for African countries because China has been filling a gap in development not being addressed by either the US or Africa's big European trade partners. But there are also high costs. For example, many Africans complain that when the Chinese take up a project, they come in with everything, including employees, and populate the area. They do everything themselves and don't include locals. And often the new residents open small businesses and shops filled with cheap goods subsidized by the Chinese government. Local African businesses aren't able to compete, and they get pushed out. So while the leaders are making deals that supposedly benefit the country, in reality, the masses suffer.

Around Africa and the world, the role of the Chinese in Africa has become a growing concern. I'm not here to say they're all good or all bad—the truth is somewhere in the middle—but the fact is China has become a dominant player across the continent. The US has a lot of catching up to do to keep from getting squeezed out.

Stemming the Tide of Radicalization

Radical militant groups, like ISIS, Boko Haram, and others feed on anger and desperation. When people lack basics like food, clean water, and education, and when they perceive that their land and resources are being exploited and stolen, those negative feelings are a natural byproduct.

Much of US involvement in Africa is military and security-based. This might seem like a necessary response, but it doesn't address the root causes. The way to defeat these groups is by taking away their supply of new recruits. You do that by taking care of people and giving them an opportunity to simply live and have the basic comforts that many in developed countries take for granted.

I believe that US businesses, with the backing of the federal government, have a big role to play in changing this dynamic and providing real economic opportunity and development in Africa. This can create goodwill and help ensure security both in Africa and stateside.

Fighting Climate Change and Avoiding a Humanitarian Crisis

Global climate change affects everybody, and many Americans want to be leaders in fighting it. Even though Africa's emissions are nothing compared to many other regions, it is in many ways the front line of the fight. If the continent is primarily developed by people who are only out for money, who don't care about pollution or sustainability, that will have a huge impact on the acceleration and severity of climate change.

Despite the resistance by some in the US to acknowledging the reality of climate change, most people realize it's a grave threat that must be addressed. For businesses this is also a threat. If you want to have a profitable long-term investment, you need to be thinking about fighting climate change so that it doesn't destroy whatever you're developing (in Africa or anywhere else in the world).

But development in Africa can be done in a sustainable way—which can have an equally big impact on slowing or mitigating climate change and potentially save millions of lives of those most at risk. That could come in the form of clean energy production, sustainable agriculture, electric cars and public transportation, protection of water resources, or many other green solutions. In America, we have some of the best technology for solar and wind energy. The top place to sell most of that equipment is in Africa—the untapped market potential is outrageous.

The US is a leader in the world—but it's not leadership by just making money or fighting military battles. It's leadership by example. Most US companies, because of the ethics of American business, are not going to a place to take and destroy and disregard the people. That's the nature of the ethics of this country, and it's what leadership is all about: adding value and promoting sustainability, both economic and environmental, to build a better world for all.

If You Can Dream It, You Can Do It

I know that for a lot of people in the US, the thought of doing business in Africa seems impossible. But I'm living proof that "impossible" is just a state of mind, and when you see an opportunity that's so incredible, you can't let the fear of difficulty get in your way.

For me, coming to America and getting an education was such an opportunity. I've now had a successful law practice for over a decade, and so many times, people have told me how extraordinary my own journey has been. Early on I didn't realize it myself, but, when you have people point it out to you, it really hits home.

My law colleagues used to remind me all the time. When I started out, I shared an office with two great guys, Tom and Chris—two all-American guys and successful lawyers—super sharp, with big hearts. They would tell me, "You don't even have a clue...the things you've done in this country, most people born here never do."

Going through school, I had two kids and a stay-at-home wife. I worked full-time and went to school full-time. I finished my undergrads in under three years and went straight into law school for another three.

I came out and passed the bar the first time. When I told those guys, they were shocked— "How in the world could you do that?"

To me it was just doing what I had to do. But they kept reminding me, "This is not normal. You know, we were born here and grew up here. We know the hell we went through going to law school. How could you be from Cameroon, come here, work full time, do school full time with your kids, and then pass the bar the first time?!"

That helped boost my confidence, and it also showed these more experienced guys that if they helped me out, I would have something to give back. So we developed a great, mutually beneficial relationship which opened some important doors for me.

So how does this relate to working successfully in Africa? There are two main points:

1. If you see an opportunity and want it bad enough, and you're willing to do whatever it takes, you can succeed despite all challenges.

2. For the best chance of success in any new venture, it's important to have mentors and guides who know the environment you need to operate in—positive relationships with people who can partner with you and open the hidden doors you'd never even know existed. That's what I'm here to offer.

The Key to Succeeding in Africa

So to close out this introduction, let's take a quick look at what you need to succeed. We'll explore all of this in more detail, of course, but I want to start helping you view this African opportunity as a perfectly solvable challenge.

1. Find a trusted partner who knows the culture and can make sure deals are legitimate and projects are done professionally. Fraud is common, and trust is low, so you can't rely on the first person you meet who tells you they'll help you do what you want to do. It takes experience to know how to read between the lines and get things done right.

2. Don't just work with the governments—work with local people. Most US businesses, especially larger ones, just deal with the central governments, but many of those leaders don't care about doing what's right for anyone but themselves. If you can show the people you're benefiting them, and you're not just there to take, they'll stick with you and protect what you're doing.

3. Do things above board and leverage the power of the US federal government. A lot of shady deals go on around the continent, and yes plenty of them involve Americans looking to make a big score. But when things go wrong, they have no one to turn to. There is so much money to be made doing legitimate business in Africa, and so much benefit to having the US government behind you, that it makes zero sense to go through back channels.

Africa is a battleground. And the world's future will be shaped by how this beautiful land and its people is treated and developed in the coming years. This book is your entryway into a land of cultural and financial riches. Let me show you how to get there, and create a lasting legacy for a better world.

Chapter 1

The Africa Opportunity

What's happening in Africa is the greatest economic revolution in the history of the world. It's already well underway, but it's also still early enough for you as a business owner or investor to shape its direction, help people, and profit.

Despite the rapid economic acceleration of the past two decades, Africa remains vastly underdeveloped in many areas, presenting a massive opportunity for those willing to take the plunge *and* do it in a smart and ethical way.

Part of the opportunity is to make a positive impact in the lives of millions of African people currently getting ripped off by unscrupulous profiteers. Rather than being carried by the wave of economic development sweeping the continent, the poorest are getting left behind. Poor Africans lack access to basics like water, decent housing, and electricity... all the while sitting on trillions of dollars' worth of resources and millions of acres of farmland that could not only ensure no African goes hungry, but also feed the world.

However, I'm not suggesting you should invest in Africa out of charity. Africa has received a ton of charity, and it hasn't solved the problems. What's needed is real development and economic opportunity that provides for the people, not just the elite. What I am saying is, where there's a big problem, there's a big opportunity, and you can profit in the process of helping people.

Africa: Reality vs. Perception in the US

A lot of people in the US are ignorant about Africa. I don't mean that as an insult, just as a statement of fact—ignorance simply means a state of not knowing. For most Americans, if they think of Africa at all, it's a vague impression of a backward, wild place, rife with corruption, political strife, poverty, and violence.

Jerome Ringo, Goodwill Ambassador to the Pan-African Parliament, has traveled extensively throughout the continent, working closely with leaders and seeing firsthand the reality for everyday Africans.

"I've made nearly 80 trips to Africa, and the greatest realization I've experienced is that everything I was ever taught about Africa, up to my first trip, was either wrong or a lie," Ringo explained. "People in the West tend to see Africa as an unintelligent, antiquated, poverty-stricken continent that has its hand out for help from the rest of the world but does not have the ability to stand on its own two feet. The perception has always been that Africa is represented by babies with swollen bellies and flies crawling out of their mouths."

It's not that Americans don't think there could be potential there. They just don't know much about the place, and they've been fed a certain set of images about Africa that do not exactly elicit confidence from a business perspective. For businesses and investors, other than in natural resources, it's not on their radar...or if it does come up, the attitude is that it's too complicated and risky to even consider.

And I get it. If you run a company or have cash to invest, you're looking at opportunities for making money that match your knowledge and your risk tolerance. You're not considering a place that seems plagued with trouble after trouble. So that's why I decided this book needed to be written—to raise the level of knowledge about Africa and show ways to make investing there less risky.

Most business people aren't recognizing the size and potential of the African market, and at the same time they're stuck with some outdated assumptions about the riskiness and difficulty of the business environment.

And to me, that's the mindset that has to change. How do we expand our thinking? There's something going on here that's going to shape the future of global business and culture. It's time to take a closer look at this place and have somebody that does know what's going on break it down for you. You're welcome.

Where There's Need, There's Opportunity

Africa is a vast and diverse place, with 54 countries of greatly varying size and economic power and thousands of tribes and cultural groups. It's hard to sum up "what is happening in Africa" or "Africa is like _____." Some Africans don't even like to hear people talking about "Africa" as if it's one place, while others of us recognize that we have certain commonalities despite all the diversity. As you'll see shortly, there are significant efforts underway to bring more unity and solidarity to the continent, but talking about it as a whole remains difficult.

So with that caveat, this book is my best attempt to open up a useful conversation about what *is* happening across the continent, and what *should* be happening. The biggest issue is lack of development, across the board: infrastructure, finance, education, you name it.

Despite the natural riches all around them and under their feet, millions of Africans live in poverty, without access to education or opportunity, subject to famine, wars, and the worst impact of natural disasters and climate change. They lack infrastructure of all sorts, and even their water resources are drying up. We'll explore these needs in detail in a later chapter.

Mouchili Mayoua, a senior infrastructure specialist in Senegal, offered this perspective: "The conversation about Africa is shifting from one of "deficits" and "gaps" to one about opportunities, prospects, ventures, and creativity. There is no place comparable to Africa where entrepreneurs and businesses with ideas and an appetite for risk can bring value and find long-term growth if they are persistent, creative, and determined."

Let's briefly look at just a few areas where development is lacking… and where creative entrepreneurship can make a huge impact.

Electricity

Most of Sub-Saharan Africa (SSA) is lacking in adequate, reliable electricity production and delivery. For example, the entire country of Benin has only one city that's significantly electrified. One. That's Cotonou, the economic center. The rest of the country, meaning roughly half the population, is essentially without electricity. And where do they get their power in Cotonou? From Nigeria, which has some of the largest blackouts in the world. They have the biggest population and economy in Africa now, but they themselves don't have reliable power. South Africa also has some issues with electricity, even though they've been a "developed" country with a large economy for a long time.

Some African countries are trying to use natural gas to generate electricity, or even gasoline. So, we're trying to stop climate change, but people are using these energy sources that add to the problem. And maybe they have to use them right now, but I don't think that's the best way of going about it. I would say, bring in the best solar and wind, and if necessary sell the fossil fuels to people that really need it in the short term to make money to develop their country. But don't invest heavily and build a ton of expensive infrastructure for these unsustainable resources.

Energy is huge, because it's needed for everything else. I see renewable energy as a huge opportunity. There is so much sun and wind energy available, and US companies could be the leaders in bringing light, literally, to Africa.

Transportation

The energy needs tie into transportation too. For example, think about cars. Even though they have so much oil, Africa has some of the most expensive gasoline in the world. That's part of the reason a lot of people don't own cars—they can't afford to put gas in them. And anyway, I can see the end of oil. People don't want to believe it, but it's inevitable.

Electric cars, that's the future. Whoever figures out how to bring cheap electric cars into Africa and develop the infrastructure to support them is going to rule. When the technology advances enough to produce electric cars that cost $10,000, they would sell out instantly. And there are cars right now that cost $10,000 in the US, but they run on gasoline. Imagine having electric cars affordable for everyday Africans—it would raise the standard of living for a lot of people. They would love to own cars and not have to burn gas. And as of this writing, Chinese company Kandi is almost there, preparing to offer its electric vehicles in the States, with budget models under $15,000.

Beyond cars, Africa has a widespread need for roads, electric vehicle infrastructure, rail, and efficient public transportation. The Chinese have been taking on these kinds of projects, but unfortunately, there are issues with high levels of debt for these countries as well as a lack of quality in many of the projects. So there's a need for better, more reliable options for this kind of infrastructure development.

Finance

For most of SSA, the financial system is very informal, which makes economic development more difficult for people. In many places, Africans don't put money in the bank—they have nothing to do with banks or even access to them. Everything is paid in cash, and often between individuals. Most villages don't even have supermarkets. People buy their fruits and vegetables from next-door neighbors. Even shoes are bought from somebody on the street who doesn't put money in the bank. He puts it somewhere in his apartment.

In the US, we're very accustomed to working with credit cards and all kinds of loans. Credit is on the rise in Africa, but most people don't have access yet. If they do, interest rates are extremely high. Most people don't know what it means to have a mortgage. If someone "owns" their home, they own it outright. It might be very simple, but it's theirs. The situation is different in countries like South Africa and in the north, where they already had a well-established system. But most of SSA is shut out of the formal banking system.

Interestingly, mobile fintech has spread throughout many countries, enabling people to send and receive money through their phones, but even that is more akin to cash than banking or credit. It's been an incredible innovation that's dramatically improved people's lives, but more such innovations are needed to bring financial tools, resources, and understanding to the masses.

GivePower Foundation is a nonprofit specializing in solar energy installations for developing areas around the world. With many projects completed and under way across SSA, they've come to know the economic environment only too well. As Executive Director Barrett Raftery explained, "There are a lot of market adaptations that are very clever, all dealing around the fact that the entire consumer base has no credit, no credit cards, no credit scores, no bank accounts, and never taken a loan." But in order to elevate these economies, more innovations will be needed, particularly in the area of financing, because as Mr. Raftery also pointed out, "Anything big is built with debt."

Water Security

With the continuing development of climate change, drought is a critical issue. What do we know about Africa? It's hot. Rivers and lakes are drying out, so many areas are losing their water resources. Most of those areas that are arid are getting worse, and meanwhile, as we've seen, the population is increasing. People are cutting down trees for fuel and to make room for farming and pasture. But without trees, the land becomes a desert, and they end up with a shortage of drinking water. How are they going to survive in the long term?

Clean water is essential for a healthy, functioning planet. As we've seen with the coronavirus pandemic, access to clean water has to be there for everyone, or we all pay the price. So between climate change and these other crises, people are finally starting to catch on, and industries are developing as a result. So this is a major, urgent need *and* opportunity.

Manufacturing and Agriculture

The lack of manufacturing and production in Africa boggles my mind. All those natural resources and agricultural products, and they just get shipped off to other places for processing, leaving most Africans with just the most menial of jobs and the barest of livelihoods.

Take agriculture, for example. The majority of Africans get their food and income from farming or agricultural jobs. The World Bank estimated that Africa's agribusiness could be worth $1 trillion by 2030.[9] As the Brookings Institute estimated in 2016: "Food production in sub-Saharan Africa needs to increase by 60 percent over the next 15 years to feed a growing population."[10] This is a huge and growing industry.

But right now, the vast majority of the activity is simply growing and supplying raw materials. Production ends at the primary or sometimes semi-refined level. But what if companies and industries started manufacturing goods in factories at the source of raw materials? That would give people a better livelihood and working conditions, raise the potential to protect the land and environment, and ultimately deliver superior products. Study after study has shown that consumers today want to see that the businesses they support are having a positive impact in the world. There's nowhere like Africa to do so much good for people and the environment while at the same time making good money.

Untapped Human Resources

One main reason Africa is the hottest area in business today is its huge, young population hungry for opportunity. Africa has always been known for natural resources and agriculture, but perhaps its greatest resource is its people. They are the world's new workforce, and given the opportunity, they excel in every area. African immigrants in the US, for example, tend to be highly educated and successful.[11]

At the moment, professional skills are lacking due to insufficient education and training opportunities, but businesses can turn this around. Take Samasource, for example—one young woman's passion and vision turned a sleepy Nairobi internet cafe into an international data processing powerhouse, which has grown to provide jobs and training to thousands of poor and marginalized Africans.[12] Large companies too, such as GE, have found great success in nurturing top-performing professionals through dedicated training programs. The human capital is there; they just need the chance to develop.

We've now looked at just a few high-level examples of the needs and opportunities in SSA. We'll be digging into these and other areas more deeply, but I hope you're starting to see that Africa is the final frontier in global economic development, and that entails everything you can think of.

So now you might be wondering, what about the business environment? Isn't it complicated and backward? Well, let me inspire you with some interesting changes that have been taking place to make SSA a more attractive place to invest.

New Developments Changing the Business Game in Africa

Africa is in a process of regrouping. One of the big problems for business in Africa has been fragmentation, not just country-to-country, but regionally. This goes back to colonial days—Africa has operated under a legacy of colonial sections established by the French, English, Portuguese, Spanish, and Dutch.

And still today, Africa is divided into economic regions. You have ECOWAS, the Economic Community of West African States, which is 15 countries tied together—Nigeria, Ghana, and others. CEMAC is made up of central African countries, including my home country Cameroon, which is now the biggest economy and supplier of goods in the region.

On the positive side, you could set up in one country and quickly expand into the same industry in the other countries in the region. In CEMAC, we're looking at a population of almost 37 million people, just within this region.[13] Any breakthrough started in one country could expand to the next. This is especially true in industries where other investors aren't looking. Everyone's eyes have been on oil and gas, but there is so much low-hanging fruit in other areas. Someone with the knowledge and resources to grow a business can become a dominant player across a whole region because it's one economic system.

Free Trade Across Africa

Now, here's the big change coming—an open market for the entirety of Africa. The African Union recently created a free trade zone, meaning if you produce something in any African country, you can sell anywhere else in Africa without restrictions, tariffs, customs, and all the current complications. This is a *huge* deal—in fact, the African Continental Free Trade Area (AfCFTA) is the largest such area since the creation of the World Trade Organization.[14]

Ambassador Ringo was the only American present at the signing of the agreement in 2018. "Africa now has positioned itself to become a real player in the economic picture of the world," he said. "As opposed to many separate economies, now you have a single economy that has a GDP of somewhere around $3-4 trillion, which will make Africa the sixth largest economy in the world."

Part of why this is so important for the US is that even since African countries achieved independence, the European countries have in some ways protected their former zone in Africa. The French, in particular, never truly left—they exert a huge amount of economic and political control in those countries. These regional economic zones have created barriers that make it difficult for newcomers to get in. For anything you might want to do, there are already companies from France or the UK that are already hold a dominant position.

If you look at Francophone Africa—Cameroon, Gabon, Senegal, Niger, Chad, etc.—they have one currency, which is the France-backed CFA Franc. So where's the central bank of these countries' money? It's France. Think about the amount of money the French make off this African currency.

So it's a game-changer that the African Union has come together to break down those barriers and have a free trade zone within Africa. Instead of the US trying to compete at a disadvantage with European countries, investors will find it easier to challenge them. And you can set up in one country and expand to serve the entire continent. So for US companies, it's cutting down some of the barriers to entry into Africa and taking away some of the control the Europeans have had for centuries.

This should incentivize companies to actually establish themselves there, instead of just having some kind of satellite or collateral operation. It's more worthwhile now, because instead of just serving one small country, you can serve the entirety of Africa. When there's free trade, you can get it done.

Moving Toward a Single African Currency

At the same time, there's a move toward a single African currency, akin to the Euro. This will take time, but there has been significant movement to set up a single currency for ECOWAS, one of the main economic regions in Africa. Some see this as a major step toward a single currency for the continent. And even if it only affects the one region for now, that still removes a lot of friction for having a business operation that covers all 15 of the member countries.

This is a major step they've been trying to take for years. Implementation was supposed to take place by 2020, but moves by the French as well as complications due to the coronavirus pandemic have slowed progress somewhat. However, they're closer than they've ever been, and if it proves successful, we'll likely see other regional organizations do the same.

So imagine if in another decade or two you have a pan-African Free Trade Zone and a single currency. The flow of business will be incredible! It will make trade or business import/export very easy. It also helps in the sense that, when you are within Africa, you don't have to struggle with all the exchanges. So if as a US company, you want to invest in any of those countries and then later expand into others, you don't have to worry about what it's going to cost you everywhere. You'll be able to put reliable numbers on it. You could more easily assess and measure your investment. If you have one currency, you can see the flow of money in and out, and you can see how stable it is, to predict future earnings.

In the old days, you couldn't really know, because how do you even value the money? In 2008, inflation in Zimbabwe topped 500 *billion* percent[15]—after printing a Z$100 trillion note, the country was forced to abandon its currency and allow citizens to use money from other countries.[16] This was due to fallout from President Robert Mugabe's forced land redistribution policy and subsequent suspension by the UK and US sanctions. The situation got better for a while after they tied their currency to the US dollar. But then the currency changed again, and in 2020 inflation once more began spinning out of control.

This is an extreme example, but it's certainly not a unique one. It's easy for one leader or one foreign power to damage a single country's economy and currency. But it's much harder if you have a single currency across a large region—if there's an effect, it's going to affect everybody. When you have a shared currency, there's more incentive for everyone to keep it more stable.

So with these changes, a business could better forecast the long-term financial impact of its investment. We're not there yet, and it may be some time, but you don't want to wait until everything is set up. By then all of these markets will have also been developed by someone else. A little risk now, played intelligently, can reap big rewards.

A Need for Better Development Options

It's also important to look at things from the African perspective to understand the potential there. Africans are wanting more economic inclusion. They feel stuck with one foreign colonizer after another, working in tandem with corrupt government officials. They want better options—true partners for true development.

To give you a little historical perspective, I grew up in Buea (pronounced Boy-yah), Cameroon. It's a historic town, right by Mount

Cameroon, which is the second largest mountain in Africa. The Atlantic Ocean is right behind it. It's a beautiful place.

When the Europeans first came, it's one of the towns that was strictly occupied by Germans. So it has a very strong German influence in terms of infrastructure. It's funny, if you ever go to Cameroon, you will not see any relic of the French or English, who came later. There's nothing that they left. You can see what the Germans before them left behind—buildings still in existence today, like they were built yesterday. It's a shame what happened with World War II and Nazism—before all that, they really had done some good development work.

Now the Chinese are all over Africa, and what they're doing, unfortunately, is often a lot more like the French, or worse. There's a sentiment among the people that China and other eastern companies are just the latest set of exploiters, there to take. They make a show of providing development and infrastructure, but many Africans feel that anything the Chinese are providing is primarily for their own benefit. Yes, they are building a lot, but the deals are opaque, they're prone to corruption, and the quality is often low. So who knows if anything they're building will last even five or ten years, let alone a century?

Africans are waking up to what feels like a trap and a scam, and they are demanding better options. So the key for Americans is to go in with the intent to add value. That would be a big and refreshing change. That's not what most of the Europeans have done. They come in, get the gold, diamonds, minerals, oil, etc., and take off.

Now Africans are wiser, and the world is very close. There's mass communication and social media. People see more of what happens. If there's a mine in some village, someone is there with a cell phone taking pictures of kids digging in the pit.

I think American businesses are the perfect partners to provide better options in many industries. They have the potential to lead the transformation of Africa in a positive direction, and get a lot of benefit in the process. By being good stewards, they can realize huge growth and profits.

Leading on Sustainability

And the implications go beyond Africa, extending throughout the world, by adding energy to the global push for environmental sustainability. The 2019 UN Climate Action Summit saw significant advancement toward a carbon neutral future and a green economy.

The closing press release quoted UN Secretary-General António Guterres' final remarks: "'You have delivered a boost in momentum, cooperation and ambition. But we have a long way to go...We need more concrete plans, more ambition from more countries and more businesses. We need all financial institutions, public and private, to choose, once and for all, the green economy.'"[17]

There's an opportunity to fight climate change in Africa by developing it in a sustainable way. And although the US has been divided on this issue, most Americans want to be leaders in creating a thriving global environment. To be a leader means you promote renewable energy technology, and the key region for doing that is Africa.

The Chinese are largely seen as being there to do whatever they can for themselves in terms of money and global influence, without regard for the people or the environment. Take for example the South African Energy and Metallurgical Special Economic Zone (EMSEZ), a vast processing facility for metals being developed in South Africa's Limpopo province.

"Despite a global move towards cleaner energy, South Africa still continues to flog coal," the *South African* complained. "The Chinese-controlled industrial plant will contain at least 7 metallurgical processing plants. According to a report by Business Insider, the 4600-megawatt coal-fired power plant's sole purpose is to electrify the industrial zone."[18]

This area of the country has a scarcity of water, and this special economic zone will require huge quantities, putting the people who live there as well as agricultural operations at serious risk of water shortages.

I think most US businesses have ethical standards that do not allow them to ignore the needs of the people like this. With a US company, there's a sense of responsibility, and almost every top company abides by principles of doing good. I know they're far from perfect, but compared to many other countries, I see US companies as being generally fair. And in fact, in 2019, *Business Roundtable*, an association of CEOs of some of America's leading companies, released an updated "Statement on the Purpose of a Corporation," with a focus on working not just toward financial profit but toward "the benefit of all stakeholders – customers, employees, suppliers, communities and shareholders."[19] This statement, signed by 181 CEOs, represents a radical shift away from the old paradigm of serving only shareholders and the financial bottom line, and the implications are massive.[20]

I believe stepping into a place like Africa, US investors and businesses can set an example and a standard for other companies to follow. And when you come in doing things right, as we'll discuss in this book, you come in with the power of the US government and the goodwill of the people behind you.

The US Needs to Rethink Its Supply Chains

Supply chain security and optimization is another important consideration in thinking about the dynamics between China, Africa, and America. China has already begun looking to Africa to offload manufacturing—as costs within China itself rise, Africa becomes an attractive source of cheap labor and land.[21] So why should the US go through China to get access to African production capacity when we can go straight to the source?

And of course, now we have the coronavirus pandemic effect, which has wreaked havoc on the global economy, especially supply chains coming out of China. The pandemic should serve as a compelling reason why the US and other developed countries should look to Africa for their supplies. China goes down and takes everyone with it because it's the factory of the world.

Why not establish in Africa? It has so much to offer. Raw materials are readily available and cheap. Labor is also cheap, and people are ready and willing to receive training for anything you want to produce. And I would argue there's a strategic advantage in that African countries are not going to be a competitive threat like China. They have no interest in world dominance, so US companies can be more secure and have more control over their costs and intellectual property. With so many reasons to stop relying on China, and so many advantages in Africa, I think it's about time US businesses reconfigure their supply chains.

So at this point, you should start to have a sense of why Africa represents such an important opportunity right now at so many different levels: financial, environmental, and social. It's the perfect time and place to grow a business, profit, and do real good in the world. Unfortunately, American businesses and investors aren't exactly champing at the bit to get into Africa, and next we're going to look at why this hesitancy is unwarranted, and why it's actually urgent that we change our thinking and get moving.

Chapter 2

Why NOW is the Time for US Investment in Africa

Things are changing fast in Africa. If you want to get involved, you have to create a solid plan and do your due diligence, but you can't take so long planning that you miss out on opportunities that others are seizing.

Sometimes you have to act even when you don't feel completely prepared, or you end up missing out. This is something I learned early in my career. In 10+ years as a practicing attorney, I've litigated many cases at almost every level of court in the country. But it all started with jumping on a single, big opportunity.

When I was just a few months out of law school, one of my professors called me, saying, "I need your help. I'm sending a case out to you."

I was shocked. "What? Me?!"

"I need you to represent a company that's been wrongfully roped into a lawsuit. I trust you. I want you on this case. I'll get you all the documents—study up, do what you have to do, and get ready for court."

I hesitated, "...I don't think I can say no."

"You can't!" he laughed. "Just do your research. You'll be fine. Go and get this case."

And, you know, I was scared, but I had to go. This professor and I had a bond. You have to understand, when I went through law school, I was working full time and had a family. His classes had been in the evening, and I was always in a hurry at the end. Boom, I'm gone.

So one night he stopped me on my way out and said, "Sometimes I like to stay back and speak to students, and you're always gone."

I told him, "Yes, because I cannot stay. I have a family to support. I have a job. If I lose that job, I lose my home, I lose everything. I may not even be able to drive to school. I have to do what I have to do."

And funny enough, he smiled and said, "You are my guy! I understand that 100%. You know, I went to night school too because I had to work, and I had a family." He called us the lone wolves.

So when he trusted me with this case, I could not let him down. I got to work. It involved an IT company and a small-town government that had hired it to install a wireless system. The company had hired subcontractors to do the wiring and other aspects of the project, and, let's just say things didn't exactly go well. They had serious issues, so the city sued the original contractor, then the contractor pulled all the subcontractors into it, and one of them didn't show up. So there was a default ruling against this subcontractor, meaning they had to pay a huge amount of money—hundreds of thousands of dollars, which would have put them out of business.

The owner of this company thought, rightfully so, that they had nothing to do with the issue. So I went in to fight that ruling. The court overturned it, and we won the case. Being my first time in court, it was huge for me. I was just happy that I was there, and I survived, sweating right through it.

Since then I've had a million contract cases, but just saying yes when opportunity came knocking is how I got started. If I hadn't jumped on this chance, my whole life would be different. A lot of attorneys spend their whole careers and never get the chance to head up a case in a courtroom, and because of this moment, I've been able to build a highly successful career as a litigator.

But the point is not about me. The point is that the African opportunity is knocking now, and not just opportunity—I would call it necessity. This book gives you the key to unlock the door.

Ignore Africa and Your Business Will Lose Out

If you want your business to be in a position to compete and stay relevant in the coming years, it's not just a good idea to go to Africa. It's an imperative. You have no choice, because Africa is where the economic center is shifting. You must have something to do with the continent. Any company or business that is not involved in Africa is going to disappear in years to come, or at best play second (or tenth) fiddle to their competitors who own the African market.

Why would I say that? Because it means you'll be cut off from the largest and most rapidly growing market in the world. In 10 years, we're looking at over 2 billion people, and these are young people, many of them educated and hungry for a good life. They love luxury. They're not going back to the old status quo of war, political upheaval, and social despair. People right now are going from zero to middle class. They want good cars. They want to live in good homes. They want to be healthy and to live a healthy lifestyle.

So it's the size. It's the population growth. It's the untapped resources and potential. You could walk into Africa with the shirt on your back and become a millionaire in no time, if you know what you're doing and how to operate there. There's no industry in the world that cannot be developed in Africa. If you're not part of it, you're out. The African Renaissance is on.

Learning from the African Mobile Phone Revolution

The US has been ignoring this last chunk of the world's untapped market because of the misperception that it's too much trouble and people don't have money. The truth is there are needs that people in Africa will spend every dime they have to fulfill. We talked earlier about mobile phones. It's a perfect example of how much Africa can actually change the world. The way mobile phones got into Africa is brilliant, because it reached every single person down to the smallest village. They might have nothing else, but they have phones. Even if they don't have food to eat, they have a phone.

Consider the population and think about the providers of mobile technology—imagine how much they're making today in Africa. And US companies are now cut off from that market. Not only that, but due to mobile phone access, other industries have developed that are becoming huge, such as mobile health and financial services. And those are also largely dominated by non-Americans.

In recent years, digital financial services have given millions of Africans the ability to conduct financial transactions where there are no banks, using simple mobile technology. The World Bank estimated in 2018 that 66% of Sub-Saharan Africans didn't have traditional bank accounts or relationships.[22] But in 2019 there were an estimated 747 million mobile phone sim connections (about 75% of the population)[23].

So how do people conduct financial transactions? Through their mobile services. That's why there is a rapidly increasing mobile finance industry. Here's another World Bank stat: from 2014 to 2017, mobile money was a main driver of financial inclusion in SSA, with the percentage of adults with a mobile money account reaching 21% (almost doubling). Meanwhile the percentage with accounts at financial institutions showed no growth.[24]

Incredibly, this mobile revolution in Africa is already old news. M-Pesa, the first mobile banking service (that has now changed the money game across Africa), launched in 2007, and by 2011, half the population of African was using mobile phones.[25] When M-Pesa started, people weren't even using smartphones, just regular old-school cell phones (and that's still the case for many). Now blockchain technology is generating new and innovative ways to create economic inclusion for Africans. This is the kind of innovation that has been going on around the continent as it develops straight into the digital age, bypassing many ways of doing things that more developed countries have cycled through in the past few decades.

So this shows you the kinds of opportunities that have emerged in Africa in recent years, and how creative businesses and investors have been experiencing incredible growth as a result. Companies are getting very smart. "How do I sell to people in villages where they don't have traditional or formal financial structures?" In answering such questions, they're creating industry-disrupting solutions. The longer you wait, the more time you give out-of-the-box thinkers to create and capitalize on solutions that meet the demands of the growing African population.

Reasons US Companies Don't Invest in Africa

So you might be wondering, if Africa is such a hot place for business right now, why aren't more US businesses there? I think there are a few reasons, which I hope you'll see in a moment aren't all that valid.

Americans Simply Don't Know What's Happening in Africa

First is simply not being aware of the opportunity. In America, we get fed a largely negative image of Africa, focused on corruption, disease, conflict, poverty, and any number of problems. And these issues are real, but we're not getting a balanced picture that shows the progress, or the positive potential of the continent. So unless you take the time to look beyond the common headlines, you'd never know what's going on there. Fortunately, you have this book now, so you can overcome this hurdle (as long as you keep reading!).

Americans Lack Knowledge of the African Environment

Even if the average US business owner or investor had an interest, they wouldn't know where to start in considering expanding into Africa. The rules are different. The cultures are different. The languages are different. However, just like me learning how to navigate life in America, joining the bar, and everything else I've achieved, with a can-do attitude and a knowledgeable guide, you can avoid pitfalls and achieve amazing success.

Instability

Africa has a reputation for political instability, conflict, corruption, and general unpredictability. But governments have been more stable in recent years, and many companies manage to operate successfully even where there's conflict. With due diligence and proper support, you can choose safer areas and mitigate your risk. And in this book, I'm going to show you exactly how to do that.

Lack of Development

The very conditions of underdevelopment that create a lot of the current opportunity can also appear as huge obstacles—such as the lack of infrastructure for communications, transportation, power, and banking.

It can seem like a catch 22, where the lack of everything that needs to be developed is also stopping companies from going in and fostering development. What's needed is a little resourcefulness and ingenuity, two hallmarks of American business. Everything might not be set up the way it would be in the States or other developed countries, but where there's a will, there's a way.

"It's too late."

Some experts have been warning for years that China is gaining a competitive advantage in Africa due to the vast size of their investments and their lack of ethical concern for bribery and other forms of corruption. However, even though China and others have made large inroads, they've barely made a dent. Africa is still in its infancy in terms of development, starting almost from scratch compared to what it could become.

The US has a pivotal role to play. Its systems, values, and laws align more with Africans than other countries' do. Africans share the American ideals of economic freedom, capitalism, and education. Many are not happy with Europe because of the history of colonization and the perception of ongoing political and economic manipulation. And many are not happy about the Chinese. But most Africans love the US!

So, there should be an advantage there for US companies. And with the recent changes in US government support for overseas business development, now is the perfect time to jump in. It's still early in the game. But it's a game that's moving at a very fast pace.

Thinking Long-term, Acting Short-term

In Africa, you have to think both long-term and short-term. It's great to have a big vision, but you also have to think about speed, even if it means starting smaller. For instance, I was talking with a group of startup founders strategizing about working in Africa. They were at the initial phase of raising money. They had an innovative product and a good network of contacts, but I could see holes in what they were doing, and they were taking a long time to plan and deliberate.

After listening for a little while, I said, "This is an interesting long-term plan, but what are you going to do about the short term? You're sitting and planning and holding meetings. But other people are over there acting right now. While we're here talking, the Chinese are there pushing their agenda. In the areas they're establishing themselves, it's going to be very tough to compete."

It was like these guys were loading a big steam ship trying to get to Africa. In the time it would take to get there, a competitor has jumped in a private jet, landed, done his deals, and is one his way back. It's too late.

Africa is moving, and you need to get on the fast track. There are smart people taking action and cashing in right now. The group I mentioned was looking for $75,000 buy-ins from investors, but they were looking at long-range returns. If you have $75,000 and you know where to go and how to operate, you could walk into a lot of African countries right now and turn that into half a million dollars in short order. If you're trying to raise money, a lot of investors want short-term returns. They don't want to think 10 or 15 years out. They want to see results now.

So I told this group, "So why would someone invest $75,000 when you're not sure when your venture is going to take off? Instead of holding meetings and going over numbers, stop deliberating. Leave the boardrooms and get on the ground because you're wasting your time. You're doing all this because you want investors. No, go down to ground zero, pull up your sleeves, and act now."

US Business Needs to Act Now or Lose Out to China

The US is a superpower not just because of military might—it's always been because of its *economic* power. The US has fought wars it didn't win and gotten stuck in conflicts that have gone on for years. But the one area where it's never been defeated is economics. Going back to the cold war, the US was able to come out on top through economic power, not military might. 2020 has provided a major challenge to that economic strength, but to date there is no nation on earth that's competed with the US economically and won. But China is perhaps its strongest contender ever. If things continue as they have been, in just a few years, China will be on par with the United States.

China Gaining Economic Dominance in Africa

The Chinese are pouring money and people into Africa at previously unthinkable levels. For years now they have been positioning themselves, consolidating in areas where the US could have been present. If America misses out on a population of over a billion people (and the fastest growing in the world), the effect of that is going to be enormous down the road.

As CNBC reported in late 2019, "US-Africa trade has dipped in recent years, while China is now Africa's biggest trade partner…the combined total value of African trade with the US in 2017 was just $39 billion, making it Africa's third-largest trading partner…The value of China-Africa trade in 2017 was $148 billion…"

The article also cited a $1 billion "Belt and Road" African infrastructure fund and a $60 billion aid package. And it quoted Tibor Nagy, the US assistant secretary of state for African Affairs, as noting that when African countries had opened their doors to investment, "'the only person standing there was the Chinese.'"[26]

This speaks to the investment vacuum that has existed in Africa, which China (and now others) have been rushing to fill. The Europeans were the dominant force in the past, but many Africans don't trust them after a couple of hundred years of colonization and exploitation.

The Europeans are not as powerful as they used to be on the continent (although they do still hold a lot of influence, as discussed in Chapter 1). You go into the Francophone countries, for example, and many people don't want to hear about the French any more. They've had enough. This has opened doors to other players.

That's why China is jumping in and taking advantage, as are India, Russia, and others. Many Africans are scared, but they prefer these alternatives to the Europeans, or to nothing. And many African leaders prefer dealing with the Chinese, because they don't feel interfered with.

Mailyn Fidler, a fellow in New America's Cybersecurity Initiative, noted in an article for the *Council on Foreign Relations* that some African leaders have described westerners as "conceited" and "ignorant of our conditions," whereas the Chinese take a more straightforward business approach.[27] Unfortunately, the main topic of that article was about the Chinese bugging of the African Union (AU) headquarters, so maybe they're not as straightforward as some leaders might like to think.

The Chinese are incredibly adaptable—they can work in any environment, and because the country has become so powerful, it can also compel others to adapt to it. For instance, they don't have any conflict with the Arabs, even though they have been persecuting Muslims in their own country. It's a serious issue, which many European and other countries have condemned. But not one Arab country has said anything against China on this issue, and many have even supported it.[28] Strange, right? China is too powerful and the strategic agreements they have are too important. So they find their common ground and don't try to interfere with each other.

Massive Infrastructure Development—Who Benefits?

One way China has been making inroads is by taking on large projects for free. The AU headquarters in Addis Ababa is a great example—they built it for free. This is a humongous complex that cost $200 million. That was in 2012. In 2018 they announced another $31 million grant for a new ECOWAS headquarters.[29] They use these gifts to build trust and get special treatment for all kinds of deals. They're telling Africa, "You see?

The Europeans used and exploited you, and they still are, but we're here to help." But what are the real costs?

One possible consequence is China having easy access to sensitive information from African governments. Around the same time the ECOWAS headquarters deal was announced, French newspaper *Le Monde* broke the story, mentioned above, alleging China had bugged the AU headquarters and had been siphoning off private data from its servers every night for five years, copying it all to servers in Shanghai.[30] Both the Chinese government and the AU denied the allegations, but it certainly raised questions in many people's minds.

Quartz Africa reported that the AU had subsequently taken various steps to ensure data security, like installing new servers without Chinese involvement, and sweeping the building for microphones or other spy hardware.[31] And the *Financial Times* reported that it had obtained confirmation of the hacking, while also noting that two Chinese firms have built most of Africa's telecom infrastructure.[32]

Bad Deals for Africans

Other issues tangled up in these cozy relationships are that many African countries have gotten into dangerous levels of debt with China and entered development agreements with questionable (at best) benefit to the local people. One example is a massive port development deal in Tanzania. This would turn a handful of quiet fishing villages and a stretch of pristine coastline into one of the biggest ports in Africa. It would also include a special economic zone with an entire planned city, comparable to the Chinese port city of Shenzhen.[33]

With such large-scale projects in the works around the continent, as well as many already underway or completed in recent years, China has been establishing a very strong position throughout Africa. Combined with the vast amounts of debt African countries already owe China, it's easy to see why some people fear Africa being turned into a "Second China." African people are aware of the ways Europe has hurt them, and they don't want to be exploited a second time, so they are very wary of the Chinese.

However, the Chinese government is very smart. Often, "private" Chinese companies enter deals in Africa with direct government backing. That's intimidating—I can tell you the Chinese are spooking many Africans. People don't know how to say, "No. Stop already." But when they hear the Chinese are taking on another project or deal, the feeling is, "Oh no, here we go again."

Another complaint about Chinese involvement in Africa centers on extraction of resources, from minerals to fish—bringing in huge trawlers, for example, where the locals are limited to using whatever small boats they have. There is no way for them to compete.

There is also the issue of so-called "debt-trap" diplomacy. The Chinese government, directly, and through state-affiliated companies, has subsidized or undertaken many large infrastructure projects on credit, creating large debt burdens for many governments. And there have begun to be concerns about the appropriation of state assets when borrowers can't pay (many African governments are broke). While there are many factors that contribute to African countries' financial issues, it's estimated that over half of African sovereign debt owed to foreign governments is owed to China.[34]

Africans are starting to balk at the Chinese presence and the lack of real benefit for locals. The *Financial Times* quoted Nairobi investment analyst Aly-Khan Satchu as saying the AU headquarters hacking showed that, "'African countries have no leverage over China'... He added: "There's this theory in Africa that China is Santa Claus. It isn't. Our leaders need to be disavowed of that notion."[35]

And perhaps Africans are starting to wake up and assert themselves more. The Tanzania port plan, initially agreed upon in 2013, stalled in 2019, with President John Magufuli demanding the involved Chinese firm agree to certain development terms or cancel the project. *The Maritime Executive* reported the change, noting that African leaders are feeling pressure to make sure infrastructure projects "deliver local results."[36]

In other areas, tensions are rising, with anti-Chinese sentiment growing throughout the continent. In Zambia in 2018, for example, discomfort was growing among the population about various state deals with China. Rumors emerged of selling the state-owned timber company ZAFFICO to China and handing over control of the state power utility ZESCO as compensation for an unmanageable debt load. This led to riots and violence against Chinese businesses.[37]

All of this should signal to the US to start showing up for Africa in a new way. As Ms. Fidler noted in her *Council on Foreign Relations* article, mentioned above, the AU bugging incident, together with these other issues, provides an opportunity for the West to present itself to African countries as a more favorable partner that could help provide a check on China's growing influence.[38]

America's Advantage is Slipping—Now is the Time to Regain Its Footing

There should be a natural advantage for American investment in SSA, because by and large, Africans love the US. When I was growing up, all the kids dreamed of going to study in America. It has meant so much to me to be here, succeed, and live the American dream.

I'll give you an example—the first time I tried a case in federal court was an amazing experience. I don't know if you've been to a federal building, but just walking up to it, you get a sense of power and grandeur. You see the marshals manning all the entrances. There's a lot of security, and these guys don't play games. The courtroom itself is so grand it puts a fright in you. You know that this is a place of power, and also that it represents a pillar of this great nation.

For someone like me coming from a small town in Africa, it's even more striking. Growing up in Cameroon, I could never have imagined myself in such a place, and certainly not playing a central role like arguing a case. How do I find myself here, before one of the top courts in the United States, the number one country in the world? It's a huge leap. And this is how Africans feel about the US—it holds an almost mythical status in their minds. There is no country they would rather deal with.

But that image has been somewhat tarnished. Those who are edu-cated see that many in the US don't regard Africa well. And it doesn't help when you have the president making disparaging comments about "shit-hole countries". That upset a lot of people, and the AU even demanded an apology.[39] With the younger generation, there are more educated people now in Africa and around the world who know what's going on. So you have to recognize that today is not like the old days when most Africans weren't very connected to the outside world. You need to think about your assumptions, how you think and talk about Africa, because Africa is listening.

By the way, there are powerful Africans contributing in all sectors of the US. Think of giants like Dr. Kase Lawal, chairman of global energy company CAMAC, based in Houston. And in almost all of the top hos-pitals in the US, there are leading medical doctors from Africa. There are also top lawyers practicing before the most powerful courts in the United States, not to mention engineers and many other professionals.

Another factor hurting Africans' perception of the US has to do with practical considerations of their needs and priorities. Even though the US has provided a lot of aid and military support over the years, the net effect hasn't resulted in much improvement for most Africans. For example, I was debating with a friend of mine about China vs. the US in Africa, and he said, "Well, why wouldn't Africa go with China? What has the US done development-wise in Africa? The Chinese are building roads, bridges, buildings—things that you can see. What has the US done?"

That question really struck me, because if you have a developing country that's trying to rise, anything that's not tangibly developmental looks like it's not helpful. Now, I think his assessment is somewhat unfair, because the US *has* done a lot for Africa. Take the Peace Corps—that's been an incredible initiative for many decades now. I had a Peace Corps teacher myself when I was a boy, and we loved her. Another example is medical aid. I was talking with another Cameroonian friend who had recently come to the US, and he expressed how grateful he was for the US-sponsored medical aid station back home. It had enabled him to get the life-saving medication he needed.

I think many Africans are aware of these things, and it contributes to the positive feelings they have toward the US. And I am hopeful that with the "Prosper Africa" initiative and establishment of the Development Finance Corporation, the US will start to invest more in the kinds of development projects that will benefit everyday Africans. These programs seek to "unleash the entrepreneurial spirit of Americans and the people of African nations like never before — advancing American and African prosperity and security, supporting jobs, and demonstrating the superior value of transparent markets and private enterprise for driving growth."[40] To me, this is exactly what's needed for both sides.

However, like the startup group I mentioned earlier in this chapter, the US tends to take its time, having meeting after meeting with no tangible results. Africa won't wait for that. You have to get in and set up shop and build on the wealth that's there. That's the advantage that the Chinese have because it's how they operate. The problem is they don't necessarily use it to benefit the people who live there, which just continues the exploitative patterns started by the Europeans.

It's frustrating for me, because I can see all the opportunity slipping through America's fingers as well as the opportunity for the people of Africa. I know that some companies in the US are already benefiting— big players have their money in real estate and traditional extractive types of deals. But I'm looking at the rest of the industries that are not in play. Africa is not going to live on oil and gas (not to mention the market has tanked at the time I'm editing this). People need to eat. They need clothes and consumer goods. They need healthcare and education. They need jobs. There's so much at stake.

I believe the US is more capable of addressing these needs and winning over the people than any other country. America has the resources, the technology, and also the values and ethics to achieve the needed results. And most Africans still adore America. So there's this opportunity to collaborate with the people and to bypass what the US National Security Advisor referred to as the "predatory practices" of China and Russia.[41] Long-term, for the good of the world, the continent, and its own interests, I think the US can play a bigger, more beneficial role in the fair and sustainable development of Africa.

The US Needs to Shift Focus from Military to Economics in Africa

The last couple of decades, since the attacks of September 11, 2001, have seen the US broaden its military presence and actions across Africa (along with other regions). I see this as problematic for its relationship with Africa and its image among the people. On the one hand, it makes sense that people need protection as we see the spread of militant extremist groups across the continent. You have people like Boko Haram, who bomb churches and kill Christians and different ethnic groups for no reason, or try to force them to convert to Islam.

In my home country, Cameroon, this has been an issue for years, with thousands killed already.[42] Amnesty International conducted a special investigation at the end of 2019, finding that in that year alone, at least 275 people had been killed and others mutilated, kidnapped, or had property destroyed in countless attacks.[43]

These militant Muslim extremist groups, in collaboration with others like Al Qaeda and ISIS, are spreading in Africa.[44] They're going to zones where the West is involved. They want to get rid of the West and turn Africa into an Islamic continent, because they know if they are successful in Africa, they'll have the largest population in the world.

So this is a real issue, but I don't think military action is the best, or only, approach to deal with it. If it were, after all of the effort put in, wouldn't we be seeing a decrease in these groups? Focusing on military intervention is just attacking the symptoms, while doing nothing about the root causes. In some ways it even strengthens them.

Some critics have referred to the growing US presence in Africa as a "shadow war" which does more harm than good. In 2017, columnist Katrina vanden Heuvel wrote a piece for the *Washington Post*, decrying this US military expansion in Africa for using the "Authorization for the Use of Military Force" as a blanket justification to go in wherever they want.

She rightly pointed out that this unchecked use of military force tends to feed corruption and produce "endless wars without victory."[45]

I think this is a very accurate assessment. I believe the US could make a big difference in creating peace and stability in Africa, and while there may be a place for military support to physically counter extremist groups, that alone will not get the job done. The military just doesn't do much for the people in these countries. And in many ways, it has a negative effect, because people use their presence as an excuse to start causing a stir: "Look, they're invading! We don't want these people here!" So it feeds anger and resentment, turning potential allies into enemies, who then are more likely to side with the ones you're there to fight against. If you're building up military presence but you're not building up business, there's something missing.

Others like the Chinese are taking over businesses and the economy. China focuses a lot on government-to-government projects, as well as on making deals that ensure that Chinese businesses benefit, such as forcing African countries to promise to buy Chinese goods.

So they're giving themselves an economic boost, whereas the US is still focusing on military support.

The other main US focus—aid money—is also problematic. It's often funneled through nonprofits and businesses with terms that are moralistic, like, for example, giving health aid, but requiring African countries to adopt anti-abortion stances. The Chinese just take a pragmatic, "non-interference" approach that focuses on economics, and that's why they've become the dominant player.

One of the most modern, progressive constitutions in the world is the South African constitution, which the US was very instrumental in writing. It accommodates everybody, just like what the US stands for—religious rights, civil liberties, it's all in there. I think that's part of why, when Mandela took over, he didn't promote revenge. He respected people's rights, because they're enshrined in the constitution. So that's a good example of the US play to strengthen its values in the world, which is great. However, if that's the only thing you're fighting for, and then the Chinese are taking over all the businesses and the economy, your constitution doesn't matter.

So the US needs to take a stronger economic approach. If you develop these places, it's going to stamp out terrorism. It will cure a lot of the ills that the US is trying to help the world fight against. And it will reassert the US advantage in influencing African development. As I said, as powerful as the US military is, America's greatest strength has always been economic. The way the US can compete with the Chinese and provide the African people real benefit is by using that economic power. That's why I want the US to push for more competition—use its power to call for open bidding and rules that everybody can see. Let the Chinese and Americans put in their bid, as well as the Europeans and anyone else, and let's see who wins. On a level playing field, personally, I'd put my money on the US almost every time.

I think the US government is catching on to all of this. In addition to the new economic development policies for Africa in 2019, in early 2020 there was talk of possible reductions in US military presence on the continent. Some in the military felt this would amount to America turning its back on Africa[46], and some European officials also criticized the move.[47] However, I think that taken together with an increase in development support, it could be a step in a positive direction.

That said, the government knows it cannot turn the tide alone, which is why it's opened the doors for private businesses and investors to play a bigger role. To give you even more of a nudge, next we'll look further at the possible consequences of continued US inaction on African development.

Chapter 3

What We Stand to Lose

So far, we've looked at the reasons why in the coming years Africa will increasingly shape the world's future. Because of this emerging reality, continued inaction by the US business community could have dire consequences, both for the African people and for America, and that's what we'll look at in this chapter.

On the Africa side, as things stand, huge segments of the population are losing out. They're not only getting left out of the economic development due to lack of education and financial resources, but the few resources they do have are being threatened. Anger and frustration are growing, and crises are mounting.

But why should American business owners and investors care about unknown Africans across the ocean? Well, first, as I've pointed out, this is the market that will make or break businesses in the coming years. And I would argue that this population consists of hundreds of millions of potential customers, partners, producers, and innovators. Also, the coronavirus pandemic has shown that we are all connected, and we as a species can no longer afford to ignore unsafe conditions just because they exist on a different continent. Lastly, I believe Americans care about fairness and creating a better world, and there is a major opportunity to lead that charge, create massive goodwill, and finally do right by this incredible continent that birthed humanity.

The Many Problems of Economic Exclusion

Millions of Africans are shut out of opportunity in the formal economy. Sadly, that's nothing new, but increasingly, their meager livelihoods in the *informal* economy are diminishing, for reasons we'll explore in this chapter.

The population in Africa is growing faster than anywhere else in the world, but the infrastructure is not matching that growth. That includes social infrastructure, like education. Development and education go hand in hand, right? Technical jobs require modern skills and knowledge. But half the population or more doesn't get access to that education, and those that don't have it can't be involved in the wealth produced by all the development and innovation.

The people at the bottom need livable jobs, but without education, where are they going to find them without education? Changes in technology today happen so fast that, if this exclusion continues, most Africans will never be able to land a good job in the modern economy. So where are the jobs for the people that lack the kind of education required to take part in the modern economy? There is so much room for manufacturing jobs in Africa, but right now, there aren't enough, and the pay and conditions are often poor.

So we're going to have half the African people caught up with the world, and they're going to be okay. And of course the elite, they're going to stay rich. But as things stand, the benefits are never going to get to the bottom. So the only things these people have left—as they've always had—are the informal economy and agriculture, which often overlap. But these are slipping away too.

Issues in Agriculture

Let's consider the agricultural situation in Africa. How many farmers have the capacity to develop agricultural endeavors that are large scale and meaningful? If they had money, guess where they'd invest? They'd buy out all the land they could get, because they know that's security— they need land to grow food.

But they don't have the means, and they never get ahead because they earn next to nothing for the fruits of their labor. All kinds of materials come from Africa—corn, cocoa, palm, rice, sugar cane, you name it—but they don't have a fixed price that everybody pays.

Most of the farmers sell locally. For some products, there's no international market for them, but even items that do have a set price, African farmers are not getting it. If they went by the international price for corn and knew exactly what they'd get at a given time, just like growers in the US, don't you think the African farmer would make good money, given the lower cost of living?

But the farmers don't get to see that. They're mostly cut off from the markets, because they're not developed. Theirs are small, local, family-owned farms that amount to almost nothing compared to a typical US "family farm" that grows corn and soy on hundreds or thousands of acres with modern machinery and technology.

Buyers in Africa have supply chains set up where they come in right at the farm or in the nearby village and take the goods for next to nothing. Some are more ethical than others, but many are just ripping these people off. They send the raw materials off to Europe or Asia or America for processing and make tons of money as middlemen.

Meanwhile the African farmers have no resources, and they stay poor. Now, that used to be okay—meaning people could survive and have a decent life, as my grandparents did. But nowadays, foreign corporations and wealthy investors are buying up the lands, and either taking over agriculture or developing for other uses like mining, fossil fuels, or industry. So how are all these people in villages, and all those without education, going to make a living? How are they going to survive?

Growing Wealth Inequality—Approaching the Tipping Point

As of February, 2020 there were 20 recognized billionaires in Africa.[48] That's a lot for the continent, but I can believe that in the next 10 to 20 years, that number could easily double. That might look like economic progress to some, but what about the people at the bottom? Some of the rich are taking on initiatives that benefit the people, but the need is far greater.

This has happened in the US, too—if you look at a chart of wealth inequality, it's skyrocketed in recent years.[49] The US has been able to sustain it to some degree (so far), because we have a system in place with some infrastructure. It's not enough—lower- and middle-class people have been increasingly struggling—but it's something. And now due to the Coronavirus pandemic, the US has seen just how fragile its system really is, as most people don't have enough savings to go even a month without a paycheck. However, there's still been something in place for the have-nots, and the government has been able to provide some assistance during the crisis.

Now, in Africa, there is almost nothing for people at the bottom—zero safety net. And they're being depleted by the growing wealth inequality, the influx of foreign competition, and other factors like climate change. They live on agricultural land that's being bought up, meaning even the place where they live is going to be gone. They're going to become homeless or end up working low-wage jobs and paying rent to live on land they used to own.

Wherever big investors are not developing for industry, they'll take over agriculture. They see the value of agribusiness (remember we're talking a potential $1 trillion industry) and they want to capitalize. Right now, most lands are owned by villages or individual smallholders, but those with money to invest are coming for those lands.

One example is the Ogun State free trade zone in Nigeria, an industrial complex headed by a Chinese entrepreneur. The government provides the land, and the Chinese develop it. On the one hand, it can create some jobs, which is important, but then the locals lose control of their land. And once the investors get in, they want to keep expanding. The *Financial Times* did a great piece on this zone and Chinese entrepreneurs in Africa in general, noting the Chinese complain about "the state's inability, or unwillingness, to buy up land from local chiefs."[50] Personally, I'm glad to hear they're having trouble, but it's representative of the pressure that is mounting to get control of land from the traditional owners and inhabitants.

Now, if the locals don't have living-wage jobs (or in some cases any jobs), and they lose their lands and livelihood, plus they have no way of improving their lives, what's going to happen? I think if the situation continues to deteriorate, before long we'll see crises emerging.

Growing Anger Threatens Peace

Because of these conditions, there is rising anger in Africa, and it's a real threat to international peace and security. The US and its allies claim to be fighting terror and radicalization, but that's not a fight you can win with guns. You have to address the root of the issue by giving people their human dignity as well as economic and social opportunity.

The Changing Europe Connection

As I mentioned in Chapter 2, a lot of the anger in Africa is toward Europe. And it's not just because of the past colonization. It's being fueled by present conditions as well, including the experience of Africans desperate for a better life migrating to Europe.

In recent years, thousands of Africans have been dying in the waters of Europe, trying to get in because they're frustrated with conditions in Africa.[51] And those are the people who actually make it to the sea. *Deutsche Welle* reported in 2019 that the United Nations Refugee Agency (UNHCR) had warned that, while the sea crossing was extremely dangerous for migrants, getting across Africa to the Mediterranean coast was "far more lethal."[52]

The story doesn't get prettier for those who make it across. Attacks on African migrants and refugees have been a serious problem—large numbers of Africans in Italy, France, and elsewhere have been harassed or assaulted. For example, in Italy in 2018, following the installation of a far-right interior minister, attacks and murders of immigrants shot up.[53]

Then there's the issue of arrests and deportations. Even Spain, which had been fairly tolerant of immigration, decided in 2018 to expel 166 Sub-Saharan Africans after a large group forced their way through border fences and attacked security personnel. France also deported large numbers of African migrants who crossed over from Spain.[54]

Now obviously people shouldn't be violently forcing their way into these countries, but when you think about what it takes to get there, and all the reasons that compel them to go, you can perhaps start to understand the desperateness of the situation…and the urgent need for real change in Africa.

Militants in the Making

In the meantime, we have very angry Africans going back into Africa, saying, "The Europeans are taking everything we own, and they don't even want us in their countries." Think about it—when someone gets deported to Africa, they go back with their hearts broken, and guess who's there too meet and befriend them—members of groups like ISIS and Boko Haram. These people are ready to become radicalized overnight. And although America is farther away and so doesn't get as many African migrants, the same principle applies.

So conditions in Africa continue to worsen for hundreds of millions of poor people. Europe and America continue to do what they've done for decades, focusing on natural resource extraction, security, and aid. And then you have China coming in acting like Africa's new best friend working to develop it, but many see them as the new colonizers on the block.

So Africans feel that no matter what, they can't win. This is what fuels militant groups, and it's exactly what's happening around the continent. It takes time, but it's going to get worse if conditions don't improve for people. More will shift to the right and develop extremist views against the rich and those that are seen as exploiters.

For many, the Western countries are seen as prime culprits—Africans recognize we've been exploited by the Europeans through colonization. People feel that everything they had, the Europeans took—that Europe is built on African money. And although there's a love for America, there's also a feeling of the US being tied in with Europe as part of Western dominance of Africa. And they are demanding change.

There's a South African political leader named Julius Malema, head of the Economic Freedom Fighters, who speaks and writes extensively about European injustices in Africa. He also speaks to the burning desire among Africans for a full stake in their own destiny and inclusion in the global economic and political system. He tells it like it is, and people believe in him. He's spreading his message into other African countries and gaining followers among Africans in the diaspora, and even in Europe. In 2016, the Oxford Union, one of the world's most prestigious speaker and debating societies, brought him to give an address.

"We want to restore the dignity of the African continent, and position Africa as an equal partner in the world economy and international politics," Malema told the audience. "We want Africa to be like Europe. We don't want Europe to treat Africa like it is its own subject. Africa's time is now...not even China will be allowed to recolonize Africa. We're called Economic Freedom Fighters because we want any foreign direct investment to come...through our own terms and to the benefit of the people of Africa. This...is not just a dream but a generational mission."[55]

A Storm Brewing

If things continue on the path they've taken, we could see more conflicts erupting. Imagine, wealthy investors will own all the land, but ordinary Africans won't have a place to live or food to eat. Do you think those locals are going to sit back and allow them to farm? Or someone is mining cobalt from a village, making billions, while the people who live there don't even have drinking water? No, people will reach a breaking point. If something is not done soon, there's going to be more uprisings. I can see that coming because people will feel they have no other recourse.

The delta region of Nigeria, which I mentioned earlier, is a perfect example. Oil companies came in, put in pipes, and started taking out oil. Meanwhile, the locals are suffering—they rely on fishing, and the waters are now polluted. The fishing is gone. Everything is gone. What do they do? They resort to blowing up pipes. And that kind of reaction is never going to stop until the people start benefiting from development.

Chad is another example. They have oil coming from one region, but it's piped straight into Cameroon, over to the port, and it's gone. The people in Chad get no benefit, and many don't even realize they even *have* oil. But with communication technology and social media, people are becoming more aware.

You can see this around the world—the shift is not just in Africa, and the target is not just Europeans. People everywhere are frustrated, demanding, "Who is pulling the financial strings that are shaping our world? What are they getting from us, and why do we have nothing?"

So how long do you think this is going to last? We'll have more issues with security, continuous fighting, and a global economy dominated by fear, mistrust, and dominance rather than creating value and building goodwill. I see this as a worldwide philosophical and socioeconomic crisis, and the epicenter is Africa.

Avoiding Political and Economic Takeover

Much of the world has already caught onto the economic opportunity in Africa, and the US is behind. Every day that passes, it's getting more alarming—various countries have been consolidating so much power that, without urgent action, by the time US investors try to get in there will be no room. Africa is vast, no doubt, but these other players are positioning themselves strategically in countries that are easy to manipulate and control.

First and foremost is China. In Chapter 2, we touched on the widespread concern of Africa being turned into a "second China," and that's worth exploring further. As I mentioned, there's a gap that the Chinese have been exploiting, playing on the African anger toward the Europeans, giving false gifts to gain leverage and build trust. That's why the Chinese will come in and build roads for free.

Many don't like what the Chinese are doing, but they'll deal with them because there aren't other options. People want development, and China has brought it. Now, while I'm offering criticism of China's involvement in Africa, I also want to state that I don't see all Chinese as the same, or all bad, and I certainly don't want to encourage hostility against them, which has already been an issue. But I do see some serious issues with many ways that Chinese investors, business people, and the government are operating, and I think it's important that we have conversations about these things and look at the possible consequences.

To reflect on the mixed nature of this topic, I'll share some thoughts from my colleague Isabella Erawoc, a native Ghanaian, who has worked on the ground in Niger for some time as a logistics/procurement officer for the United Nations Migration Agency. We spoke in 2019, and she expressed some of the mixed views:

"I think that the presence of Chinese people in Africa is an opportunity. They have the advantage of not having participated in colonization. They have rapidly moved from being a developing country to an emerging country. This seems to be appreciated by Africans, who can better identify with the Chinese. Also, most of their contributions are massive, fast, and they seem to have less principle and fewer conditions...On the other hand, they have less consideration for the human condition and social protection, and this is starting to be felt in the different countries where they work."

So yes, some Africans see the Chinese as relatable, and even role models because they've already developed their own country to a large extent. On the other hand, I think the Chinese use that as a way to gain trust, even if some might just be there for their own benefit.

The Chinese come in with "free" gifts, already knowing what they want. They sign land leases for the next hundred years. Meanwhile, the poorest people are losing the few accessible resources they have for survival and getting no benefit from most deals struck with the Chinese.

Chinese Development in Africa—Questionable Benefit, High Cost to Locals

When the Chinese pick up a project, say a road, or a skyscraper, they often come in with everything to get the job done, including employees. The people in the host country get zero benefit in terms of economic development, not even from the passing on of knowledge. Some Chinese justify this by claiming that locals aren't capable of doing anything more than the most basic tasks due to lack of education. However, there are far more educated people in African than jobs for them.

"Per capita, Africans are more educated than Americans," Ambassador Ringo explained. "When you go into the airports, the people carrying your bag, most of them have master's degrees and many of them have PhDs. They are highly educated, but unfortunately there aren't jobs where they can apply their education. Foreign countries have come in and built new buildings, airports, and roads with the promise that they would use African labor. But instead they've brought in their own people, and that has robbed Africans of engineering jobs and many other opportunities." And as for Africans who do lack education, foreign investors could be training them to build and maintain these projects, however, the Chinese don't bother. This creates a justification for the Chinese to stay around long-term.

Now, the even bigger problem is that Chinese workers don't just come in to work on these infrastructure projects. They also get involved in local markets and even farms, and start to take over from locals. In fact, the impact of smaller Chinese entrepreneurs in Africa is just as great as that of the big companies and state-run initiatives.

In the US, we have people coming through the borders from Latin America, and some leaders claim they take US jobs. Many people think that's nonsense, pointing out that many immigrants work in farming and service jobs that most US citizens won't do, and others fill skilled positions where there aren't enough qualified Americans to meet the demand.

Well, in Africa, the fear of livelihood being taken from locals is not just rhetoric—it's a real concern. The Chinese come in and take over markets that the local people depend on to survive. They have the means because they have the support of the Chinese government. If you go to the marketplaces right now in many of these countries, you have Chinese stalls filling the whole place. They come in with all kinds of products that are enticing and cheap—every product you can think of, from mobile phones to shoes. That's where everybody ends up going. The local businesses cannot compete, and they start shutting down. That's exactly what's happening across SSA right now.

Even established local businesses are in danger from competition by Chinese companies. The *Financial Times* article mentioned above noted that, "...the import of cheap Chinese goods was another factor in destroying local production."[56] As an example, there is a textile manufacturer in Cameroon called Cicam, which used to be the biggest producer in the region. But it has lost most of its market share in recent years. *Business In Cameroon* reported that after a long stint at the top of the industry, "...Cicam progressively plunged to now control barely 5% of the local textile market nowadays. The reason for this is the wax prints imported from China (which represents 88% of the market officially) and from West Africa (6%) that flood the Cameroonian market at very competitive rates."[57] The article went on to note that "most of the [imported] textile products are contraband."

Another area where locals are losing out to foreigners is fishing. Coastal communities (and many inland populations too) have long relied on fishing for food and livelihood. But now large vessels from China and elsewhere roam the waters all around Africa, wiping out fish stocks. They bring in big trawlers and take huge catches back to their countries. The locals don't have those kinds of resources and equipment (and even if they did, there is only so much you can take from the ocean before there's nothing left). They use small boats, some essentially just canoes—again there's no way for them to compete. So the fishermen are losing business and a vital food resource.

Locals and experts have been raising this concern for years, but the problem has continued, fueled in part by EU subsidies and other policies, threatening the local populations as well as the ocean ecosystems.[58] *The Maritime Executive* reported in 2019 on rampant overfishing in the waters around West Africa, calling the situation, fueled by illegal and undocumented fishing, one of the worst in the world. The article noted that foreign vessels from various regions, including both the EU and China, are contributing to the problem, and that the fisheries are in danger of collapse.[59]

Many of these vessels are engaging in the illegal practice of *Saiko*, meaning the catch of juvenile fish, which is making it impossible for fish populations to sustain themselves. Furthermore, Chinese ship owners are using lobbying tactics and local shell companies, fronted by locals, to skirt the law and engage in such illegal practices.[60]

So in all these ways, instead of adding value, the Chinese are often taking it away, same as their European counterparts...but worse, because even the informal sector is now being attacked. And because the formal sector is reserved for people with education, we're going to have serious issues down the road. With all of these well-resourced outsiders taking over the farms, the markets, the businesses, the fisheries...where else can people go?

Africa On the Global Buffet

China is not the only major player in SSA. Many countries are now jumping in to grab a piece of the pie. Take Russia, for example—it has never had much of a foothold in Africa, because it doesn't have the resources. Many Russians are worse off economically than some Africans living in villages. Yet Russians have been entering Africa lately to sell weapons and develop energy deals.

In 2019, while many developed countries met to discuss adding to the UN Green Climate Fund, African heads of state, ministers, and business leaders headed in droves to Sochi, a Russian resort town on the Black Sea. There they met with President Vladimir Putin and a host of Russian officials to discuss deals for military, energy (mostly fossil fuels and nuclear), and infrastructure.[61]

It was the first ever Russia-Africa Economic Forum, and it won a variety of arms and other deals for Russia. Some experts see this as a move by Russia to present itself as a global power and ally to African countries. I wonder how much these deals are really helping everyday Africans. A colleague of mine who attended reported that many of the African representatives were dozing off during the meetings. They're just going there looking for ways to make money. Russia is very happy displaying their inferior weapons, and these leaders are buying into it.

These countries have a strong head start on America in terms of developing Africa. It shouldn't be this way, because the US has a long history on the continent, but its policies haven't kept up with the times. This is why it's so important for the US to maintain and strengthen its presence in Africa...and not just through aid or the military, but through real development. That can only happen with involvement from the finance and business communities.

Solution: Develop Processing and Manufacturing in Africa

One major solution I suggest is that American companies set up production of goods in the areas where their raw materials come from. Provide good jobs with good pay and work standards, and help take care of the needs of the locals. When the people are involved in a meaningful way and their livelihood is taken care of, they will never go against your operation because they have a sense of ownership and inclusion. But if you just take resources and use people for cheap labor, it's only a matter of time until there's trouble.

I'll give you an example: cocoa seeds. Africa is the largest producer of cocoa in the world, but chocolate isn't being produced there. Chocolate products are made in Belgium, the US, and elsewhere, but rarely in Africa. In fact, some Africans spend their life growing and selling cocoa just to survive, but they don't even know what it's used for! In 2014 a viral video showed a small cocoa producer and laborers in Cote d'Ivoire trying chocolate for the first time in their lives.[62] It's incredible watching them discover why "the whites" get so excited about cocoa.

An estimated 70% of the world's cocoa comes from Africa, but less than 1% of chocolate is made there.[63] But it doesn't have to be this way. Chocolate maker Beyond Good (formerly Madécasse), is a significant contributor to that 1%. This rare and innovative company has worked for over a decade to produce chocolate at the source of cocoa in Madagascar, and at the time of writing they've been expanding into Uganda. By developing onsite manufacturing, they've been able to create a streamlined supply chain that increases farmer pay six-fold while protecting endangered species and healthy ecosystems in the areas they work. Plus, their unique heirloom chocolate is some of the best you will find.

"Chocolate is worth $105 billion as an industry, whereas cocoa is worth $5 billion, so the raw materials are only worth so much in comparison to the finished product," Founder and CEO Tim McCollum said. "So we realized that you can actually capture more value by having the factory producing the finished product and then shipping the product to America." He added that developing more at-source manufacturing in new regions is a top priority for the company, because, "producing at origin is really how you maintain a fully transparent and equitable supply chain. That's how we've found is the only way to disrupt and change the system."

Typical working conditions in the cocoa industry (and many other industries in Africa) are notorious for issues around child labor, inhumane conditions, and lack of access to education and training. Big companies buy huge amounts of cocoa, but almost no one bothers to develop the areas where it's grown and make it a good situation for the people who live there and grow these products for the world.

And the same is true for minerals and metals. If you look up videos about so-called "artisanal mining," which sounds romantic, you find that it's just people slopping around in muck, stuffing buckets and sacks with raw minerals like cobalt.[64] They have no protective gear, not even gloves, so they're constantly exposed to toxic materials. They get paid next to nothing for the materials they collect, and they end up with serious health issues. And many of the miners are children (though the people in charge try to hide them when cameras come around). These are human beings who are just as capable as anyone else in the world, if they would just be given an opportunity to develop.

We'll return to this theme of developing manufacturing, living-wage jobs, and humane working conditions, because it's of vital importance for creating a prosperous Africa and an equitable world...and the alternative could be disastrous.

Avoiding a Humanitarian Crisis

Because of all the pressures from other countries, ongoing economic deprivation, climate change, and more, there's a looming crisis for hundreds of millions of Africans living in poverty. There is opportunity here, and it must be acted on quickly.

One key issue, as I've touched on previously, is access to fresh water. Much of Africa is arid and most of those areas are getting worse—rivers, streams, and lakes are drying out. You need water to live, and you need a huge amount of it to grow plants. Farming in Africa requires irrigation, and it's becoming more tenuous due to climate change-induced drought.

You cannot just depend on rainy seasons, because for years now, there has been a growing trend of bad seasons when the rains are too late, too heavy at once, or not enough. It leads to crop destruction and famine. If you haven't seen the movie *The Boy Who Harnessed the Wind*, which is based on a true story, check it out and you'll get a glimpse of what famine can do to a region. Meanwhile, the population is increasing, and most African countries don't have subsidies to support farming, so this is a huge concern.

Climate change, one way or another, affects everybody. But even though Africa now produces a tiny fraction of the global emissions that contribute, it stands to get hit the hardest. There have been droughts in the past when the UN intervened, sending supplies from all over the world that people needed to sustain life. If we don't do something about the effects of climate change, that's all going to look like it was nothing.

Many countries in Africa already lack drinking water. They have areas where people live off streams, which is part of why you see a lot of cholera, E. Coli, and other diseases. People upstream are using the water for many things—to bathe, wash their clothing, even toileting...and then people downstream use it and drink it, because it's all they have. So it's already a big problem, but now even those resources are dwindling. In addition to farming, you have mining and other developments that are also taking tons of water from areas that already don't have enough. It is a very limited resource.

So we know this is an issue right now. It's not a matter of if—water sources *are* drying up. So there is a humongous need. Well, how do you make sure these countries will be able to have suitable drinking water in the future when the sources have disappeared? It's inevitable that new solutions will be needed, because like it or not, that's where we're headed.

Anyone with a solution, I believe will be a winner. I think these are areas that US companies could lead and make big profits and a big impact. I mean, look at the sheer size of the continent, and almost all of it needs this kind of technology—many areas right now today, and in the next 10 or 20 years even more so.

One industry that could be huge is wastewater recycling. Whoever can get that into Africa is not only bound for billions, but they could save millions of lives. The technology exists—it's the political and financial backing that's needed.[65] Wealthier countries are doing more wastewater treatment, but rarely for direct consumption. In poorer countries like most of Africa, only a small percentage of wastewater is treated at all.

Interestingly, Namibia is one of the few countries in the world that does turn wastewater into drinking water. So there is a viable solution that could help people. Someone just needs to lead the charge to make it happen.

Another solution in coastal areas is water desalination. That's an area where GivePower Foundation, mentioned in Chapter 1, has been innovating successfully, using solar power and green filtration technologies to accomplish this in a sustainable way. Founder and President Hayes Barnard explained in a promotional video, "It started with putting solar on 2500 schools in 17 countries. And we realized very quickly that we could light up the whole village. The next evolution is, what are the most important end uses for human beings that need electricity. And we believe the number one is water."[66]

In 2018, the organization installed its first-ever solar desalination system, which provides clean water to 35,000 people per day around the Kenyan village of Kiunga, which has been in a terrible, multi-year drought. The promo video shows children covered in sores from drinking salt water, because it's all they had. Regional partner Joffy Bastard described the situation, "They had completely run out of water, and as a result they would drink fully brackish water out of wells.... We were seeing children die of kidney failure...disastrous impact on people here."[67] So getting access to clean, fresh water was life-saving, and life-changing for these people. Check out the video (link in the notes). When you see the joy on their faces just from having water, it will bring you to tears.

So, we have solutions, but so far, no one is doing enough to plan for a situation in which millions of people who already live in poverty are going to lose the few basic resources they have to survive. And as I stated previously, the resources and resourcefulness of the US business community can not only make a real difference, but it can lead to solid profits and growth...if you're willing to jump on the opportunity and take bold action.

Doing good is good business, especially for US companies. Research shows that most Americans strongly prefer buying from and working with companies that make a positive impact in the world.[68] There are so many opportunities in Africa to put this into practice and do well by helping people, yet American companies and investors aren't exactly flocking there. In the next section, we'll look more closely at some of the reasons, and some ways to overcome the perceived challenges.

Overcoming the Obstacles

I n the first few chapters, we looked at some of the excellent reasons to get into the African market. Now I want to address more deeply the reasons why more US businesses and investors aren't already jumping on the opportunity.

For many, it's just not on their radar—their focus is domestic, or perhaps working in other developed countries. For those who have even thought about Africa, there's a perception that operating there is too hard and too risky. And that's understandable given its reputation and history. However, when an amazing opportunity comes along in life, taking on the challenge and intelligently approaching the risk is more than worthwhile. I believe that if you want something badly enough, you find a way, and I'm living proof that taking on big challenges and goals can lead to great rewards.

Coming to America

The dream of almost every student in Africa is to study abroad, especially in the US. But not everybody has that opportunity, so I consider myself incredibly fortunate. That said, when you're young and dreaming of a better future, you don't always realize what that might involve. You get where you thought you wanted to be, and then you meet the challenges and the reality, which can be tough.

Getting to America was one thing. Getting settled was a whole different ball game. I had a wife and two small children, so I had to adjust and get going fast...strap on the boots and hustle like crazy. My first few jobs were actually in fast food, landscaping, a gas station—low skill and low pay. Then I stepped up to working as a counselor in a group home for people with disabilities. That was my first big upgrade, and I knew it was just the beginning.

My next breakthrough was working at a help desk center. That was a highlight of my early days in the US. The pay was better, so it helped me get ahead. Most importantly, with that job I was finally able to fulfill my dream of going to school in America.

I worked the night shifts, going in from 4pm to 2am. During the day, I'd attend classes, working toward my bachelor's degree. Like it or not, I went to school nonstop. I wanted to get it done as quickly as possible, because I felt that I was behind.

One semester I completed 25 credits. Normally, the administration would never allow students to do that. You have to have permission from the department head and the registrar. Now, if I'd had the wrong mindset, I would have thought, "Oh, there's no way." I remember when I went for the first time to meet the counselor, my only concern was finishing my undergrads and getting out as fast as possible. But she told me, "Well, since you're from Africa, you might have trouble with the language difference and difficulty of the classes, so I advise you to take at least four years, maybe more. Go slow and make sure you can keep up."

Well, it happened that she was also my English 101 professor. And when I got into her class, after a few weeks, she told me, "You don't belong here. You're too good to be here." She was looking at my grades, saying, "My goodness, why did I ever think you couldn't do it?" She told everyone, "This guy can do whatever he wants to do." Later on, she even wrote one of my recommendation letters to law school.

If I had believed her when she told me it would be too hard, I would have sold myself short: "You know what? Let me not make a fool of myself." But I was determined. I knew I just had to do really well, take care of business, and trust that everything would fall into place. And it did. I was out in two-and-a-half years and ready for law school.

So what does this have to do with business in Africa? Well, I faced a lot of challenges during that time—what I've shared doesn't begin to describe how difficult it was. But I saw the opportunity, and I wasn't about to let anything stop me. And that's the attitude I want you to adopt about the possibilities awaiting you today in Africa.

What's Stopping US Investment in Africa?

Most Americans are not aware of the potential, and they have very little knowledge of the territory. That's a major reason I felt called to write this book—to show people what is going on in Africa and what is possible.

In chapter 2, we briefly looked at some of the reasons investors and businesspeople avoid Africa. In the coming chapters, we'll examine them in more detail. I'll be giving you a window into African cultures and the business climate, so you can start to get a sense of how business works there. Of course, this will just be the most basic of starting points, but my hope is that it will whet your appetite to find out more about this amazing continent and its diversity of cultures.

Concerns About Corruption and Instability

Most people in the US would argue that there are too many sociopolitical issues and concerns in Africa—that most of the countries are unstable, leaders are corrupt, and you can't trust anyone. People don't want to put their money where the situation is so unpredictable that they don't know what's going to happen the next day.

While there is some validity to this concern, things have settled down a lot, and institutions are growing stronger in many areas, which is starting to curb the power of dictators and corrupt officials. There are far fewer wars and coups than there were in past decades. And many companies and organizations manage to conduct their business successfully and safely, even in regions where there is conflict.

The keys to success include due diligence, understanding and gaining cooperation from the people who live where you're trying to operate, and having trusted partners who can get things done properly.

Lack of Development

There's a catch-22 in Africa. The lack of all the things that need to be developed can deter companies from going in and developing. Communications, transportation, electricity, construction, and more—all can require ingenuity and creativity, depending on the location of your operation.

Lack of financial institutions and infrastructure is another factor. Financing projects can also require a different approach than you would use in the States or in other more developed countries.

And in many locations, there's a lack of models and procedures to follow. In some areas you might not find an established pathway for developing a project. So how do you get anything done? I'm going to show you how to gather support, partner with the right people, and work together to forge a new path.

Cultural Differences

Another deterrent for many Americans is the cultural differences, and it's not just one culture. There is a vast array of cultures, tribes, beliefs, and languages across the continent, as well as more general African traits and ways of doing things that differ from the US. If you've never been to an African country and you're not familiar with these things, it can all seem strange, exotic, and maybe intimidating. So we'll look at some of the cultural considerations and ways to deal with them effectively and build good relations.

In the next chapter, we're going to look at both the perception and the reality of corruption and instability in Africa, and what it can mean for you. Then in chapter 5, we'll move on to the lack of development and how to deal with it successfully. In chapter 6, I'll give you a look at some key cultural considerations. As you read, I invite you to put on your "inspired problem-solver" hat and paint yourself into the picture. What is the impact you want to have in the world? And with the right support and strategy, what could *you* accomplish in Africa?

Chapter 4

Corruption and Instability in Africa: Perceptions and Reality

Sub-Saharan Africa has a poor reputation when it comes to corruption and political stability. Its countries are young, formed from European-imposed colonial boundaries and systems. These nations have historically lacked strong institutions to protect the rule of law and the needs of their people. As a result, hundreds of millions of Africans live in poverty and lack secure access to basic survival needs.

However, within these general conditions, we can find a wide range of realities from country to country, and within national boundaries as well. For example, looking at Transparency International's *Corruption Perceptions Index 2019*, we find that overall, SSA ranks poorest for corruption of any region on the planet.[69] However, when we look country by country, we find that many SSA countries rank better than global powers like China and India, with Seychelles and Botswana landing only a few points lower than the US.

Remember, Africa is huge—three times bigger than the US, and with almost four times the population (and growing fast). It's good to be aware of broad generalities, but it's equally important to assess conditions at the local level when considering investments.

Even at the broader level, many experts point to improvements in recent years in the strength of institutions and policies that inhibit corruption. For example, Africa investment advisor Aubrey Hruby told the *Wall Street Journal* even back in 2014 that most business in Africa is clean and compliant, and that there are plenty of "serious partners" to work with.[70]

The private sector is increasingly playing a large role in solving the problems associated with corruption and making a real difference for everyday Africans. Hruby and co-author Jake Bright explained in their book *The Next Africa* that in the past, the richest people have been the politicians controlling the natural resources. But, they wrote, African countries are progressing, and the financial elite are increasingly emerging from the business community.[71] Many of these leaders are bringing a clear vision and a compelling push for a more equitable Africa, encouraging the development of stable institutions and policies.[72]

Other experts share similar findings. In *Africa's Business Revolution,* authors Acha Leke, Mutsa Chironga, and Georges Desvaux noted an emerging culture of goodwill and service among Africa's top businesses. They found that many African business leaders look at all the challenges plaguing the continent—from poverty to lack of infrastructure—as problems they feel called to address.[73] So, yes, there are challenges in regards to corruption and weak institutions, but things are changing. Clearly, more needs to be done, but before digging into the current issues, let's look at one example of significant progress.

Recognizing Progress and Addressing Realities

Transparency International's *Corruption Perceptions Index 2019* highlighted Angola for significant progress in reducing corruption. This southern African nation still ranks low overall, but it has made significant improvements after decades of authoritarian rule and a civil war that lasted almost 30 years. We're talking about a country whose entire history up until 2017 consists of breaking free from colonial control only to have one single ruler (Jose Eduardo dos Santos), with much of that time filled with war.

That war was driven by a complex mix of conflicts over natural resources, political ideologies, and personal power plays. From 1975 to 2002, with a couple of brief pauses, conflict raged between the government and a factional leader named Jonas Savimbi, who was from an area rich in diamonds and other resources.

Now, here's a question: regardless of how anyone feels about his political leanings, how could someone fight against the central government for so long? The answer is, he had support from around the world, including the US. You can easily find pictures of him meeting with US presidents like Ronald Reagan and George HW Bush. His allies gave him weapons, and they made him rich. The whole thing became a proxy for the cold war between the US and USSR, with Cuba, South Africa, and other nations also involved at various times (although the Angolan conflict continued past the end of the cold war).

Peace agreements were reached couple of times, and Savimbi was to become Vice President at one point in the 1990s. But the deal fell apart and more fighting ensued. The war didn't end for good until he was finally killed by government forces. Since then, there's been relative peace. However, there's still been the issue of alleged corruption under the former president.

So, that's obviously a very brief and simplistic look at Angolan history. The point is, it's been very troubled, so for this country to be singled out for progress by the leading international corruption watchdog group is remarkable. The new president, Joao Lourenco, has been on a crusade against corruption since taking office in 2017, firing Dos Santos' children from government positions and initiating an array of investigations. In 2019, this resulted in recovering $5 billion of stolen assets.[74]

And Angola is not alone in making significant progress toward stabilization and the stemming of corruption. Another African nation that's made surprising progress is Rwanda. This is a country that's gone from terrible civil war and genocide to being on the forefront of economic development and political progress in SSA. According the World Bank, "Rwanda has guarded its political stability since the 1994 genocide... strong economic growth was accompanied by substantial improvements in living standards, with a two-thirds drop in child mortality and near-universal primary school enrollment."[75] Of course, you can't just sweep the history under the rug in any of these countries, but you also have to recognize what has improved and look to a brighter future.

Industry-Level Improvements

In addition to looking at SSA governments, it's also useful to look at industry improvements. This is especially important because natural resource exploitation and conflict have gone hand in hand for a very long time in Africa.

One area that stands out is the diamond trade. For years, this industry was fed by blood. The entire war in Liberia was fueled by the diamond trade, as were those in Sierra Leone, Angola, and others. If a factional leader occupies an area rich in resources, and someone gives them money and weapons, it enables them to fight against the government.

That's what the terms "blood diamond" and "conflict diamond" refer to—warlords fighting over these resources. Someone rises to a little bit of power, and a foreigner supports him in exchange for access to the natural resources. These guys fight to the death. Meanwhile, the resources are being carried out of the country with no benefit to the people. Still to this day, many such places don't even have drinking water. It's sad—people just focus on gold and diamonds and "How much can I get?"

The 2006 film *Blood Diamond* made a real impact. After that, the entire world decided, "We've got to stop this." There is now a standard for rough diamond production and trade called the Kimberley Process Certification Scheme, which is meant to ensure diamonds are "conflict-free". That's an international standard—every diamond in every legitimate shop must have its origin traced. This process was developed because of the many years of war and bloodshed in Africa.

There's still a black market and fraudulent activities, but it's not as rampant—or as lucrative—as it was. So it's still not great, but it's much better. And I know we can do better still. We must. The international community needs to bring these kinds of standards to other industries and products.

Even "Good" Deals are Often Bad for the People

While we must celebrate these signs of progress, there are still widespread issues with corruption and instability in Africa, and I believe US investors can make a difference in cleaning things up further. Black market deals remain common, but even many of the more seemingly legitimate deals in Africa create negative impacts for the people.

For example, in 2019, Senegal experienced an uproar after the BBC revealed findings that the president's brother, Aliou Sall, had received suspicious payments and employment favors from an international trading company. This company had received rights for offshore oil development, even though it had no prior experience in the industry. The company, owned by Timis Corporation, then sold its rights to BP for somewhere between 9 and 12 billion dollars.[76]

People were furious. They took to the streets in protest—it was a big deal. All the involved parties denied any wrongdoing and said the BBC falsely portrayed the deal. BP said it had done its due diligence and had no record of bribes or inappropriate payments. But the people were enraged, and the president's brother ended up resigning his government post.

I think those involved knew exactly what they were doing. BP probably thought it was protected from any involvement in corruption because its deal with Timis was all above board. But you can't pretend you don't know about these things. It leads to problems down the road, as the people lose trust in foreigners as well as their own government. This adds to the resentment and anger we talked about in the previous chapter.

Another example of corruption from 2019 involved the president of Congo Brazzaville. San Marino, a tiny country that lies inside of Italy, seized €19 million from various accounts owned by Congo's President Denis Sassou Nguesso and his relatives, after an investigation into money laundering. Some of what the money in these accounts was found to have been used for included €114,000 for crocodile skin shoes, €2.3 million for watches, and €11,000/night hotel rooms.[77]

And San Marino kept the money, so those funds are gone from Congo now. If you go there, you will see the people barely have food to eat. People in San Marino have money, and its population is not even that of one province in Congo. And not only that, the money they confiscated was only part of the fortune the president had there. So for all anyone knows, the rest still sits in those accounts. It's a shame.

Some countries that find suspicious accounts will ask for proof the money came from legitimate sources. If not satisfied, they'll treat it as a criminal enterprise. The US will usually find a way to send it back, after collecting what it cost them to handle the situation. Some countries just keep it, like in this case. So it comes in, but it doesn't go out. It's like a roach motel for money.

Business, government, and finance leaders of the West need to wake up and recognize there's a heavy cost to continued complicity with these kinds of dealings. As an outsider coming in, you have to build trust by acting in the best interest of the people of these countries. Seek out and align with officials who are really trying to do right by their constituents. Any closeness with corrupt leaders can create trouble for you. You become seen as an enabler. If you want long-term, successful development, the *people* are the ones you need to have on your side, and the leaders who are really working to improve conditions for them. Fortunately, more such leaders are emerging.

Business Standards Needed to Stop Corruption

As I mentioned, a lot of the corruption that exists in Africa has to do exploitation of natural resources, and the people who provide them. We talked about improvements in the diamond industry, but diamonds aren't the only things mined in Africa. The same kinds of issues are involved with the mining of other minerals, it's just that they're not as exciting and well-known.

Take cobalt, for example. I own a cell phone. I imagine you do too. We walk around with these supercomputers in our pockets, but most of us have no idea what's in them or where those materials come from. We don't think about it. We might be aware that cobalt is a mineral of some sort, but we aren't aware of how it impacts our lives (like allowing our phone batteries to function). Or, what in the world is chromite? or phosphate rocks? The public doesn't know anything about these materials coming out of Africa. The companies that produce goods using these materials are making tons of money, but what about the people at the source? How are their lives? I can tell you that most of them are dirt poor and don't even have clean water. It's inhumane.

Child labor is also a serious concern in many of these areas. We talked about "artisanal mining" previously—if you look up artisanal cobalt mining online, you'll find videos of people of all ages bent over in shallow pools, sifting through rocks by hand. They have no safety gear, no facilities, just a muddy pit. They load up sacks with little rocks, and everyone's haul just gets piled together. People are dying of cancer because of the exposure.

Meanwhile, some buyers, usually Chinese or other foreigners, have a little shack where they pay out peanuts to these people. And when, once in a while, journalists or others come to investigate, they try to hide the kids. But there are too many, and they're out in the open, so it's obvious what's going on. Once in a while a news story comes out, but for the most part, no one talks about it because it's too troubling to deal with. And because they're not as visible, it's easy for corrupt profiteers to keep taking advantage of poor people.

Dealing with Armed Conflict

Hand in hand with the exploitation and lack of development, there is the reality of religious conflict, political conflict, and tribal conflict, which can still erupt. Radicals and warlords take advantage of any situation so they can gain power and money.

A friend of mine from Cameroon was working as a senior engineer in a large medical device company here in the US, and he decided to go back home and start his own firm. His goal was to start a small, inexpensive business and build up capital to start producing medical devices over there. So he quit his job, moved back to Cameroon, and opened up a factory to produce chicken feed.

That might not sound like an exciting business, but he's a very smart guy—went to some of the best colleges in America, and in addition to being a top engineer, he got an MBA, because he saw the power and potential of business. He had a good investment with the feed factory. After about two years, he came back to visit and said, "I guarantee you within the space of a few years, I'm going to be a billionaire." It was growing fast, and he was starting to diversify. It's a great example of the kind of plain, simple, boring little business you can do over there and build it into something significant.

Unfortunately, a political conflict developed in the area. It started out peaceful, but then it started to get violent. Petty warlords took advantage of the situation and started going after anyone they saw as an easy target, either to get money or just to show their power. My friend was operating on his own, and his shop became a target. He ended up needing to relocate his operation and start over with more partners and support.

Now you might be thinking, "Okay, Evaristus, you're talking about violent conflicts and warlords. How could a company operate in that kind of situation without risking a lot of safety issues?" I think the problem would solve itself through the presence of more Western companies creating a stronger environment of legitimate business enterprise. If they set up properly, develop these areas, and provide good jobs and access to global markets, the warlords would die out. And it would be not through violence, but through lack of funding. Because if the black market is not there, how would a warlord survive? Without the market, the warlord is nobody. If there's a legitimate business and economic environment and people are taken care of, the warlords will be gone.

There are two lessons here. First, you do have to be aware that conflicts are a possibility, so it's important to exercise due diligence and find ways to protect your investment and your people. You really have to investigate what's going on in an area and look for signs of any issues that could surface. Always assess the risks before acting.

And if you do decide to enter an area that's less stable or more prone to conflict, you have to take that into consideration as you plan your strategy. The economics and relationships are different, so having trusted partners is even more essential. GivePower Foundation, the solar energy nonprofit mentioned previously, has extensive experience in such areas. Executive Director Barrett Raftery was kind enough to share some insights from 12 years on the ground in various SSA countries:

"There has to be a premium cost placed on endeavors in these regions and budgeting to support that. They are less stable and fundamentally more risky...trusted local partners take on a truly life or death importance. Understanding the nature of conflict economies, which differ from organized international wars, is critical in understanding which projects will be protected by the community and safe, and which will be at risk. In my experience, when doing these projects, more care is needed in the planning and operations phases, and timelines are slower."

The second lesson: the US has a stronger role to play in changing the situation through real economic development, so that these kinds of issues continue to become rarer. I think US companies operating in Africa in legitimate enterprises, backed by the federal government and/or with strong support from the people, will be safe. My friend with the feed operation was an African, operating quietly by himself, and unfortunately, bad African players tend to prey on their own. He could have grown his business into something big, and I know he still will, but he was starting very small and simple and had no protection.

I think that bringing the wealth, power, and legitimacy of the US to partnerships with the local people is the perfect combination. Build a proper factory and hire locals. Work with the embassy so you have the US government behind you, and everyone knows it. You'll have protection, and you'll help make the area where you operate safer for everyone, by providing development, jobs, stability, and visibility.

Many of the companies that use African minerals and other materials are based in the US. They could decide to bring the ethics of US business to the source of their raw materials, if not directly, then by setting up new businesses entities or forming partnerships. I would like to see proper mining and processing facilities that end the exploitation of children for labor. Africa needs clean, professional operations with good wages and safety standards, with transparency so people know what's going on and they get real benefit. It would be good business practice for US companies to recognize that they could stop much of this deprivation. People would love them, both on the supply side and the consumer side.

FCPA: It's Time for the US to Change Its Approach in Africa

I believe there's a fundamental shift that must take place for both US businesses and the government, if we want to continue to have a meaningful connection in Africa. In recent years we have been losing ground, and as a result, the African people are suffering, and losing trust.

So what do I mean by a fundamental shift for US involvement in Africa? In part, I am talking again about a shift from focusing on aid and military/security support to a focus on real economic development. You can train military personnel and engage in armed conflict, but if you erode goodwill and stoke resentment, you add to the problem. America has a trust advantage over every other competitor country, but the military presence in many ways reduces that advantage.

As stated previously, this kind of US policy shift is beginning to happen with the Prosper Africa initiative and the establishment of the International Development Finance Corporation. But these moves are just a piece of the puzzle, and ultimately, it's America's business leaders that can make the biggest difference, and reap the biggest rewards.

That said, I must bring up another important policy issue that I believe needs to be addressed: the Foreign Corrupt Practices Act (FCPA). What I have to say on this matter may sound controversial, but I simply ask you to consider it with an open mind.

This is a well-intentioned law that's been on the books since 1977 and became much more prominent in the 2000s.[78] It is designed to discourage US affiliated companies from paying bribes or otherwise participating in corruption abroad. In theory, this sounds like a great idea, but its effectiveness is questionable at best. Ironically, in competitive markets like Africa, it has a side-effect of giving a major advantage to enterprises from other countries that have lower ethical standards. In Africa, over the last decade or so, the Chinese in particular have benefited tremendously from this advantage.

I believe this policy needs to be changed, and fast. "But Evaristus, how can you say you're in favor of letting US companies pay bribes?" Well, that's not what I'm saying. My view is that the FCPA is bad for US companies doing business in Africa, and as a consequence, it's bad for Africa. It's suffocating investors and companies, making it hard for them to compete. You cannot compete with such a high standard when there is no standard for the rest of the world and all the other players walk in and out freely, doing whatever they like.

A few experts have warned about these issues over the years. Back in 2011, the *American University International Law Review* published an extensive article by analyst Reagan R. Demas, which detailed the trends at the time and the impending dangers. With the drastic increase in enforcement in the 2000s, companies had begun investing large amounts of money and energy in compliance. But to what end?

"Despite this clear trend, attaining the ultimate goal of the FCPA to lower the incidence of official bribery and corruption in Africa and beyond seems no closer than it was when the Act was passed in 1977," Demas concluded, adding, "These same companies...are growing ever more concerned about the numerous other companies operating in Africa that are unencumbered by the anti-bribery strictures weighing upon US entities and foreign companies with a sufficient jurisdictional connection to the United States."[79]

In many cases, that concern has led to businesses simply pulling out and letting the competition have their run of the market. Demas reported, "Many of these companies are even ceasing operations in countries with particularly acute corruption risks, often at substantial cost and future profit loss."[80]

Unfortunately, in the ensuing decade since this publication, the situation has only gotten worse, which is largely why the US now finds itself behind the curve in Africa, while China and others have been taking over. Everybody else is heading to Africa to invest, but US companies are lagging, in part because of the FCPA.

The US is seen by many as the moral leader among the countries of the world, but it doesn't work when everyone else has the freedom to go in and do whatever they want. It only works if everybody plays by the same rulebook. You cannot have one set of rules for the US and another for the rest of the world.

How would you expect a company to bid on a contract when there is no bidding—when the other party walks in, pays, and gets the contract, and any alleged bidding is just a charade? Most of the Chinese money going to Africa is through state-sponsored corporations, so the government actually has an interest. With US companies, investments are basically privately owned and funded, without the direct backing and involvement of the government. The new federal programs might help, but I think the government should take off the shackles, let businesses go out in the marketplace and fight just like everyone else.

Survival of the fittest—don't people claim that's what capitalism is? I think the same thing should apply in Africa. Let them compete. Whoever is fit is going to survive. I think American enterprises will come out on top in many cases because they have higher ethics and quality standards, and there is more inherent trust. They will do what they have to do, but they will also do what's right, so they will be able to win against other competitors.

Some might say if the FCPA is not there, it means you're encouraging these companies to pay bribes. I will argue no—we must trust in their moral and ethical obligations to do what's right. If US businesses are free to go in and bargain just like everyone else, they won't *need* to pay bribes. Their presence alone will create a better environment. If Africans see that Americans will do things right and truly help, of course they will choose to work with them over anyone else.

Big companies like oil & gas can deal with the FCPA, either by investing enough to cover all the compliance procedures, or in some cases violating the law and paying the fine. They have been able to afford it because the profit is so much higher than the fine (although that may no longer be the case due to COVID). But that's not the right way of doing things, and it defeats the purpose. And what about smaller businesses?

There are many companies that would go in and do good work, but they don't have the means to deal with compliance or be fined so much money, when they may not even be successful with a project they're trying to carry on in Africa.

The US Justice Department is making a lot of money penalizing companies, but it doesn't benefit the host countries where the corruption is happening. So at the end of day you have to ask, "Okay, who are we doing this for? How does this help those poor countries?" It's just a show of fighting corruption, measured in dollars of fines.

It's pointless because only companies that have a connection in the US can be punished. So it's a wasted effort. It means all the other countries will take all the opportunities that are there. They're not going to wait for the US or play by the same rules. They're going to do what they have to do.

No one is willing to openly say, "You know what? Let's change the FCPA." Most experts will tow the line, saying the US companies can actually obey the law, and still do well. That's where I differ: I say, yes you *can* do well, but we should make it easier. One person who did speak out against it was Donald Trump. Back in 2012, he was quoted as calling it a "horrible law" and questioning why the US was trying to police the world.[81] I think many people thought when he became President he would try to get rid of the FCPA. But interestingly, he's left it in place, and prosecutions have continued at a similar pace through most of his presidency.[82] There has been one change specific to energy companies. A new law was about to take effect requiring disclosure of all payments to foreign governments, and Congress scrapped it when Trump entered office in 2017.[83] Otherwise, enforcement of the FCPA itself has continued.

I believe the responsibility of handling corruption should fall to the host countries. They can set up their own laws, and if someone breaks it, they can charge them. The US should allow them to do that and use its power and influence to support those initiatives.

As Demas put it, "Western countries are, on the whole, failing to use their full arsenal of weapons to attack the demand-side of bribery, allowing these efforts to play second fiddle to politics, energy independence, and national security considerations…Ultimately, the current supply-side anti-corruption enforcement environment is unsustainable, and the future of the corruption battle and economic development in Africa hinges on change."[84]

FCPA shouldn't be one-size-fits-all. It should be tailored to the various areas around the world, taking into account the realities of the situation on the ground and the ways the law can actually feed corruption rather than reduce it. The intention of the law is great. Businesses should work in ethical ways that benefit people and society, not just executives and shareholders. But the effect of this law is counter-productive in many situations. Don't let your own rules handicap yourself. You're putting the US at a big disadvantage in a continent that is the future. Like it or not, it's where everybody needs to be.

I think we should find ways to accommodate the market changes around the world. So let's not scrap it completely, but let's amend it in a way that frees US businesses. The US loves competing, but you cannot be in the boxing ring with your hands tied, competing with these countries. China is not small. Russia is not small. We should untie the hands of American businesses and let them compete.

Leveling the Playing Field

Some experts who agree that we need to level the playing field espouse that the way to do that is to keep calling for higher standards from competitor countries like China. I think that's great in theory, but how do you enforce that?

You can posture all you want, but you can't tell China what to do. If there's no enforcement mechanism, you're wasting your time. That is the biggest flaw with this law, because enforcement is only against entities that have a connection in the US. If a Chinese company with a base in California is involved in a corrupt act, they can actually face penalties here in the US following the law. But most Chinese companies are going through the Chinese government, and they aren't subject to this law? If a Chinese company has no link in the US, there's nothing anyone can do.

It's the same with Russia. They are in all the worst places you can think of with arms deals. How do you tell Russia, "You have to abide by this." We can't even stop them from meddling in our own elections and culture with their social media troll farms.

So if we were only dealing with competition among Western countries, this would be the perfect law, because they will enforce it. They would follow what the US is doing. But what do you do with the rest of the world? Something has to be done. Pressuring other countries to adopt higher standards sounds great, but until you can enforce it, it's a waste of time.

Other experts claim that there is actually a rise in global anti-corruption efforts, centered around the Organisation for Economic Co-operation and Development (OECD).[85] One of this organization's main focus areas is anti-corruption globally and bringing countries together, which again *sounds* great.

However, what countries are involved? To become a member of the organization is very tough. You have to go through a serious process. China is not a member—they're listed on the website as a "key partner," but it's unclear what that means and how involved they are. None of the BRICS nations are members. Nor are any African countries. None of these countries qualifies for membership because they're too corrupt. You have Chile and Mexico, and Colombia just joined. Otherwise, it's mostly developed, Western countries that are members, so it's another old boys' club.

It's good, but for whose good? They're trying to stamp out corruption, but from where? I don't think there's so much corruption in Denmark or Sweden. So what corruption are we talking about? If you want to target Africa and try to stamp out corruption, but the people that are actually the stakeholders are not included, what can you hope to accomplish?

I think a better way to level the playing field would be for the US government to use its power and influence to change the game on the ground. First, in a lot of African countries, the US embassies could push for open bidding on contracts. Right now, there are a lot of closed-door deals going on, and the people who pay to play are the only ones invited in. I think the US needs to confront this issue to support transparency and competition. Say to African countries, "Look, you want to stem corruption, but you're allowing people to come in and take contracts without bidding. Let's have open bidding."

I also think the federal government could accomplish more by changing the way it funds projects. The US sends a lot of aid money to African countries for projects that never end up getting completed. So I think that money could be better spent paying reliable companies to get these things done. If there's a dire need for electricity, or healthcare, or water infrastructure, and there's a US company that can supply or develop it, why don't we do everything we can to help them?

Instead of sending money to the country, only for it to disappear with nothing accomplished at the end of the day, why don't we pay the provider so we get projects done right? Companies here can do so much. They have the expertise and the resources. All they need is financing and a pathway to get in and get the job done. And we know if we pay them, we can trust them to follow through.

It's time for the US to reimagine how we deal with the corruption, instability, and lack of development in Africa. We have to recognize how our own policies and behaviors are hurting rather than helping, and make changes today. That said, US businesses and investors should not wait for the change to come from the government. We have to find our own ways of doing things, like working with trusted partners, leveraging the new political and economic changes in Africa, and recognizing "boring" opportunities that others are ignoring. We'll be delving into these areas and more throughout the remainder of this book.

We All Have the Power to Change Things

We all have a part to play in fixing the instability and corruption issues in Africa, because we've all contributed to them in one way or another. Much of the corruption ascribed to Africans is fueled by opportunistic foreign entities, both from the East and the West. We need to own this reality and raise the standards by rethinking our strategies. I believe the US must change its approach to have a stronger and more positive impact, and in doing so, we can realize incredible financial rewards while leading the world forward in a sustainable and humane direction.

Chapter 5

Finding Opportunity in Africa's Lack of Development

The underdevelopment in Africa scares off US companies because they have to operate differently and think through logistics that are already established in more developed regions. But the opportunity is worth it, because right now you can get in on the ground floor. The alternative is to wait for China and others to develop everything, but then they'll have so much control and influence that you'll have to go through them to do business.

So in this chapter, we'll take a look at how we can approach the lack of development in various areas as an opportunity to do good through smart investments. Just as we looked at perceptions versus reality in the areas of corruption and politics, we also need to have better clarity about the state of development in Africa. While the continent remains stunted compared to what it should be by now, there has been a lot of economic growth in the last couple of decades.

For example, there are many more large businesses in Africa (over 400 enterprises at the billion-dollar level) than most people realize.[86] But even at the lower level, there is a lot more economic activity than was previously accounted for, which is becoming more apparent as the informal sector morphs and becomes more connected to systems that allow for tracking.

On the other hand, in some ways conditions have gone downhill for those on the lower end of the economic scale. We need new approaches to turn things back around for them, as well as to meet the needs for jobs and economic opportunity for the growing middle class.

The Erosion of Progress

I was born in a pivotal time in my home country of Cameroon. Independence had occurred in 1960-61, and the country was still finding its footing. However, whereas you might think that 50 years ago, the state of infrastructure development must have been incredibly primitive, in some ways it was better. Plumbing, electricity, and roads were actually quite good, and economically people were comfortable. It goes back to all that the Germans had built prior to World War II. What they left, to this day, is still functioning.

We had a very good hydroelectric system. We had good roads at the time—just major roads linking in one city to the next. They didn't go into the villages, but they were good. There were good hospitals. People had enough to eat. We went to school. I had a fairly comfortable childhood in terms of basic necessities.

Of course, there were some families that struggled, but I don't remember people laying on the streets begging as I saw later on. Growing up, we never knew there was such a thing as people begging for food or money. For most people, it was subsistence farming, plus a little bit of commercializing to make some money. That's what my grandparents did, growing all the common tropical foods—coffee, cocoa, plantains, etc. They did okay, and all of their kids went to school.

Those who didn't farm were civil servants or teachers, or they ran little mom and pop shops. But people made it—things were good enough for people to live. It's strange that this could change. With the regional conflict the last few years as well as the growing economic inequality globally, some people are really struggling these days.

This situation is not unique to Cameroon. Across the continent, post-colonial authoritarian governments failed to build on the development work begun by the Europeans. Now with the explosion in population and the growing demand for economic inclusion, we are reaching a point where continuing in this manner is simply no longer an option. So in this chapter I'm going to show you some of the areas where development is lacking, and how savvy business people can turn those deficits into opportunities.

Areas of Needed Development

Despite all of China's efforts in recent years regarding infrastructure projects and other development work, the vast majority of SSA remains underdeveloped. Let's look at some of the key areas ripe for American investment and ingenuity.

Transportation and Construction

First is physical infrastructure of all kinds, from transportation to construction to utilities. Most of what exists in Africa today is old—it's what the colonial masters built in the early part of the 20th century. And some of the newer works are poorly constructed, as with some of the Chinese projects.[87] There's a need for quality, modern design, engineering, and building in almost every SSA country.

Take roads, for example. That's a top issue. Africa is mostly agrarian, and most agricultural products are found in less developed areas, right? They're not in cities. But if there are no decent farm-to-market roads, it's much more difficult and expensive to transport those products to the consumer or the ports. If a farmer lives 100 miles from the nearest sea port or airport, how can they transport perishables to the market before they spoil? The shortage of good roads hampers economic development.

Right now it's tough for farmers. And that's one reason a lot of farming has remained at the level of subsistence only. They cannot develop to the next level that's required for actual economic value in the secondary sector. If they had affordable and viable access to the larger markets, they would have more opportunity to develop larger operations.

Rail transportation is also lacking and needs to be developed. If a country has quality railways and roads, people can transport goods from one end to the other without issues. But those assets are almost nonexistent compared to what is needed for people to thrive economically.

You don't have to run a huge company to facilitate these kinds of projects. For example, Beyond Good, the chocolate company mentioned in chapter 3, has helped build roads (as well as schools, wells, and other projects) in their areas of operation in Madagascar. "We try to make it a collaborative effort," Founder and CEO Tim McCollum said, "So we'll try to gather in other organizations and also have the village or city that we're working in gather whatever resources might be needed to facilitate a specific project. The impact is huge, and it's awesome to see how excited people get about these projects."

Electricity

The lack of electric power is definitely one of the top issues across the continent. As of 2019, the average access to electricity in SSA was a pitiful 43%, less than half the global average of 83%.[88] As with everything, some countries are doing better than others. There were actually 16 countries with less than 25% access, including Rwanda, which is held up as a model of progress and development.

Without power, all the rest of development is arrested. Nothing can operate. You need power to run any larger operations, from mining to agriculture. And if you want to transform those primary products into something, you need to be able to power those factories.

Today with innovations and new technology, we have all kinds of inventions that could help, for example new types of hydroelectric systems that are quicker and easier to install and don't require dams. However, with waterways drying out, other solutions will likely be needed as well. The latest technologies in solar and wind energy point the way to the future, and Africa has plenty of both.

Renewable energy—that's a need in almost every SSA country. Nigeria is a huge oil and gas producer and is the biggest economy in Africa now. Why don't they have electricity? Right now, as I'm writing this, part of the country is dark—zero power. Why don't they have solar or wind power there? That's a big opportunity.

Groups like GivePower, mentioned earlier, are doing great work in this area all over the world. And Ambassador Ringo, as Founder and Chairman of Zoetic Global, is also an entrepreneur in green technologies. He has focused on renewable energy as well as energy efficiency. For example, the company has introduced an eco-friendly freon replacement that can cut energy costs by 40%. This offers another avenue for development, because lack of refrigeration is another major hurdle across SSA.

"Over half of the medicines shipped to Africa spoils, and the same is true for food grown in Africa, because there's no cold storage," Ringo said. "If we can create systems that reduce the cost of refrigeration and create more cold storage capacity, that will directly impact the agricultural industry. The hope is to help Africa become a net exporter. They have more than enough growing capacity, but they need to be able to protect their perishable products."

More such innovations are needed, and they're needed at scale. US businesses should be jumping into this market.

US Missing Out on Renewable Energy in SSA

The Chinese come in with inferior equipment and get all these projects. This is one area especially where I cry for the US, because there are companies here that could go in and make a tremendous change. For example, I have a colleague who got a contract to supply a certain voltage of electricity in Cameroon. He had everything set in terms of the agreement with the government, but he didn't have anyone with the technology to do the project.

So he was talking to a Chinese company. That's exactly what happens all the time. Now, why isn't he talking to anyone in the US? Because outside of oil and gas, the US has its eyes closed. The rest of the industries are sleeping. They're not available or even interested. They'll hang up the phone because they don't know who you are or anything about your country. When they hear Africa, it's like, "What? Where?" Maybe they assume it's some kind of scam, or it's just not on their radar.

Even for me, it can be hard to make connections. I did some outreach for this friend, as well as for another who had a contract for renewable energy in Benin (which as noted previously has almost zero electricity production). I found some solar energy companies and contacted them. Believe it or not, nobody wrote back, nobody called, nothing, even after I followed up. And I'm here in the US. So my colleagues in Africa don't have access to the US. They don't know what companies are here. They don't have contacts. If they reach out, no one pays attention. They don't have examples of companies that have done things within Africa that they could turn to and say, "Can we do the same in this other place?" The US has great suppliers for renewable energy, and it's time they start paying more attention to the vast demand they could help meet in Africa.

Manufacturing

Africa is becoming the next and final major hub of manufacturing. If developed well, by ethical companies, this could significantly uplift the economic wellbeing of the African people. Think about all of our computers, mobile devices, rechargeable batteries—a lot of the raw materials to make them come from Africa. Those finished products could also be produced there, and that would create industries that dwarf the oil and gas so many in the US focus on.

This ties in with mining, which we've looked at previously, but it's worth mentioning again. A lot of the mining in Africa today is very primitive and poorly organized: economically, environmentally, and operationally in terms of safety and working conditions. So companies creating goods from those materials could get involved at the source to improve the conditions for mining and resource extraction as well as provide manufacturing jobs.

Why hasn't any of this happened? For all reasons we've been considering—the lack of technological knowhow, the lack of infrastructure, concerns about instability and risks. But really it just comes down to most companies either not seeing the need and benefit or not having the will to make it happen.

But for those who do rise to the challenges, the rewards abound. Beyond Good has realized a variety of benefits from having an integrated supply chain. The strong, positive relationships with suppliers and workers who are competent, empowered, and invested have been quote beneficial, especially as the coronavirus pandemic took over the global economy.

At the height of the global lockdown in spring 2020, McCollum reflected, "It has given us a big advantage to be able to allocate and manage the necessary resources to continue production. While we have minimal production happening and safety procedures in place, chocolate is still being made daily in Madagascar. By having control, we are less vulnerable to the impact that these types of events can have on a supply chain."

It's unfortunate that Beyond Good is such a rare example of this kind of thinking. Africa is looked upon as the farm to the world, but in most cases, the crops are just harvested and shipped away. There's virtually no processing or production, which removes most of the money Africans could make from their natural products. They don't get the benefit of the whole process.

I want to see more of these full supply and production chains developed and operated in Africa, so the people are getting paid for more than just raw materials and the back-breaking work that goes into producing them.

So I would suggest that consumer goods companies look at Africa. Look at the triple bottom line. You want to make money, do something meaningful, and help the planet? Get into the market. The farm is right there, so set up your factory and maybe even some of your marketing or operations. There is cheap labor for everything, and people are hungry for learning and opportunity. If you treat them well, you will create tremendous loyalty and goodwill—these people will fight for your business.

Agriculture

There are many other needs and opportunities in agriculture and food as well. Take chicken, for example. Right now, it's a luxury good in SSA.

People don't eat much chicken in most of those countries. There's just not much supply. Poultry farms are generally few in number and small in scale, so it stays expensive.

In many village areas, if people eat meat, it's often from what they call "bush meat animals"—they hunt whatever they can find, which is not easy. Another thing that's eaten in certain areas is snails. For the most part, people do not eat much meat. It's saved for special occasions, such as one chicken for the family at Christmas. They eat mostly beans or legumes for protein, because they grow all of that locally.

But many people would love to have other options if they could afford them. The US has great models for raising livestock efficiently but also cleanly and humanely, and we need to apply those skills in Africa.

Education

One of the biggest complaints by companies trying to work in Africa is that there's not enough skilled labor. This is a confusing situation, because on the one hand, as mentioned earlier, there are a lot of educated Africans who can't find good jobs. But on the other hand, Africa doesn't have enough high-quality schools that train people for skilled jobs. The curricula of most schools don't cover what's needed in business today. However, if there's a skills shortage in any particular area, Africans are perfectly capable of learning. This is another area where Americans can make a huge impact.

I mentioned Samasource earlier. It has had great success training people in IT and data jobs, evolving into one of the world's leading companies for training and validating machine learning. And since launching in 2008, under the belief that "Talent is equally distributed, but opportunity is not," they have provided meaningful income and poverty alleviation for over 50,000 people, many of them in SSA.[89] GE is another great example. It has set up an extensive training program in Nigeria, as well as launching an e-learning portal at the end of 2018.[90]

You don't have to be a giant company to teach people. Virtual education has really started coming into its own in recent years, and since coronavirus hit, the growth has been exponential. There's almost no limit. You could be set up in one small office and target companies from any industry you like to provide training for whatever they need. In many trades, people can be trained in a matter of days or weeks.

Think about call centers. People used to get annoyed off when they got a rep on the line in India, because of the accents. But guess what? Businesses didn't give it up. Everybody's used to it now. Well, how about Africa? In many areas they speak better English than most Indians. In Nigeria now there are people who speak like Americans. There are plenty of Africans that could easily be trained to do these jobs. Education is a widespread need across the continent, and America has some of the best trainers and educators on the planet. Sounds like a perfect match, right?

Finance

Now, we should ask, *why* do all these countries have a shortage of electricity, not to mention education and infrastructure? Think about it—they have rivers, they have lakes, and they have lots of sun and wind. Why haven't they developed enough power? There are many reasons, but one of the biggest impediments is lack of financial systems.

Finance is a major issue across SSA—the lack of access to credit, banking, and the global financial markets. For example, the capital market in Africa is almost nonexistent, so it's difficult to raise a large amount of money for development projects. There aren't many banks per capita to begin with. Then, most of those that exist are not liquid enough to carry on big projects. Many aren't even liquid enough to do basic lending.

GivePower's Barrett Raftery shared his insights on the financial realities, saying, "The combination of very few credit worthy entities, no real credit scores, very little banking...all of these risks have made Sub-Saharan African countries experience extraordinary interest rates over their lifetime." He described the conundrum for potential investors: "You can struggle to get any loan for anything in an African context, and then when you get the privilege of having a loan, you're paying 12% interest. Why are you going to build infrastructure there?"

GivePower has so far gotten around the issue of lack of credit among its projects and recipients by leaning heavily on grants. However, the organization is looking ahead to innovations in financing to create broader, more accessible solutions that can scale. He explained, "We think that the way forward is to underwrite projected cash flows—instead of the credit score—of the off takers and leverage the prepaid methods established by the telecoms to deal with low-credit customers."

Creative financial developments like this are sorely needed across Africa, and I believe American finance experts could make a major contribution.

Tourism

Tourism is another key opportunity area. It's hard to know what tourism will look like in the coming years due to coronavirus, but at some point, in some way, it's going to come back. Africa has some of the best tourist sites in the world: historic areas, incredible landscapes, beautiful pristine beaches, and much more. The islands like Mauritius and Seychelles have been doing well from tourism, and Kenya has benefited because of its wildlife. But there are so many opportunities that are not yet developed.

For Americans, hotels could be a great area to invest—clean, modern, four- and five-star facilities to serve both the growing African moneyed class as well as tourists and business people from abroad. Those structures don't exist in many places right now. The middle class is coming up and more people have money—they want to have nice vacations and stay in quality hotels. Many Europeans vacation in Africa as well. Now is the time to take advantage of the growth.

A great example of this is Bob Johnson, an American businessman and investor who founded Black Entertainment Television. He built a 5-star resort on the beach in Liberia back in 2009 that attracted a lot of attention and signified a new era of peace, coming just a few years after the end of a long civil war.[91] There are areas in Africa that investors have not gone into because of security and because it's not developed. But Mr. Johnson is someone who saw the opportunity and bought ocean-front property to build quality accommodations. There is much more room for these kinds of developments around Africa, both coastal and inland.

I think many people would also love to see a major high-end hotel chain that has an African brand and locations in all the top spots around the continent. That could be developed through a partnership between Americans and Africans, and I think it would be an outstanding success as well as create more economic opportunity for Africans.

And of course when we're talking about tourism development, we must think not only about luxury. It's important to consider preserving all the natural elements, landscapes, waterways, and wildlife that draw people. Because if those are lost, not only will it have negative environmental consequences, but why would tourists keep coming? Americans have the ability to think about these long-term considerations and foster tourism infrastructure in a sustainable way, which would be very welcome.

Secondary Sector/Consumer Goods

We talked about manufacturing, but I also want to highlight a specific class of opportunities that I believe has limitless potential in Africa. And that is all the consumer goods cottage industries that currently make up the informal economy, which still dominates a lot of the continent.

Most US investment in Africa has come from large companies in the primary sector, with a heavy focus on oil and gas. But the secondary sector, in particular consumer goods, is just waiting for people to come along and ramp it up. There are incredible business opportunities that could serve the domestic African population, but to many Americans they might sound boring.

For example, one savvy businessman came into the area where my family lived and set up a factory to produce detergents and soaps. He started supplying hotels as well as individuals, and within two years, he controlled almost the entire area market. Those soaps were all anybody was using at home. They were different for Cameroonians, with a more pleasant scent than what people were used to. They were excited that this American had come to set up his operation and bring these modern products. I had cousins that worked for him; everybody was jumping on board.

There are still many opportunities like this across SSA. Those types of businesses right now are mostly small and inefficient. But with American technology and business knowhow, they could start to scale and take advantage of the growing demand.

Analysts aren't paying enough attention to these industries—their gaze is fixed on oil and gas, natural resources, technology to some degree...the more popular and exciting industries. I'm always looking at things that we take for granted but people in the less-developed countries do not have. There are so many areas that business people in the West don't notice, because such goods don't mean anything to them. To me, because of how I grew up, they're a big deal.

Right now in Africa, this kind of industry can be a money-making machine if it's approached intelligently while also raising the standard of living. And the cost to get going can be relatively low. Take, for example, the chicken feed startup mentioned earlier. That was a self-funded operation that saw immediate growth. Whether it's clothes, food and beverages, household goods—you name it, you'll find unmet demand as well as ready labor.

Low Costs, High Impact

With so many resources, so much demand, and plenty of low-cost labor, Africa presents an array of opportunities for business investment. You can set up production near the source of raw materials, create products at the lowest cost, and sell anywhere you want.

Africa is the final frontier in manufacturing. Europe used to be the manufacturing hub of the world, but these days it's mostly service-oriented because it couldn't compete with lower-cost markets. The US has been going down the same path—a lot of outsourcing to other countries in recent decades. Some of it has started to come back in the last few years, but nothing like it used to be.

And now even in China the cost of manufacturing has risen significantly compared to 10 years ago. Other Asian countries have gotten into the game and started producing even more cheaply. But that's not the end of the story.

As an investor, you want to look for where you can produce at a lower cost compared to any other place and beat the market. The focus now should be Africa. It will have the lowest cost in everything you want to do, especially given the fact that the actual raw materials that you need are right there. Just the cost savings of transportation alone are huge. If you're willing to train people for manufacturing, they're willing to learn. Millions of Africans are ready to join the workforce. They just need the chance.

Some analysts argue that labor costs in Africa are not actually that low, especially compared to some parts of south and southeast Asia. But they're generally factoring in the perceived costs of the other aspects of African business we've been discussing—security, instability, infrastructure, skilled labor, government policies, etc. These can make it seem that the cost of labor would be cheaper in some Asian countries than in Africa. But if we have ways to mitigate those costs, as I'm suggesting in this book, and we can look at labor outright, you will not find a cheaper source.

Reputation Boost

In addition to the financial rewards, companies that invest in African development will have a lot to be proud of—making a lot of money, and creating jobs. For most Africans, to have good-paying jobs, it would be an incredible transformation from what's happening now. You'll raise their standard of living, and they'll have money to spend on other products, to save, or simply to ensure they have decent housing and other necessities.

Research has shown over and over that American consumers love to buy from companies they see as doing good in the world.[92] And that could be part of the marketing for your company. "We are changing lives in Africa and thereby uplifting the world." This will also prevent people from trying to immigrate to look for jobs. Why leave your home and family if you have what you need?

Opportunities abound in Africa, and I want to help you get there. Success requires understanding the people and working with them to create mutual benefit, so in the next chapter I'm going to give you a crash course in some basic African cultural considerations. We'll look at both the macro level as well as the importance of understanding the specific cultures and people anywhere you might invest.

Chapter 6

A Brief Introduction to African Cultures

When many Americans think of Africa, they imagine vast stretches of open land and small villages with "primitive" ways of life and strange tribal cultures. Many also think of poverty, armed conflict, and famine. These are all certainly part of the picture, but it's a mistake to think of such themes as the essence of what Africa is.

The truth is both more complex and, at the same time, simpler. By complex, I mean that Africa is a huge continent with 54 countries and thousands of tribes, languages, and customs. All of it has been shaped by a tangled and painful history of colonization and exploitation. On the other hand, when I say the truth of Africa is also basic, I mean that it's a continent filled with human beings—and despite the variations in customs and ways of life, in some fundamental ways, humans are the same everywhere. And viewed through the lens of our common humanity, you'll find that Africans are more like you than you might expect.

It's important to look both at the commonalities that bind us together as humans and the cultural nuances that can come into play, for better or worse. The cultural differences can seem like an obstacle for Americans used to working in developed economies, but seeking to understand the culture you're dealing with can provide the keys to successfully working and investing in Africa.

Africa: A Historic Cultural Crossroads

Let's start with a little bit of historical perspective. Consider this for a moment: before the Europeans came into Africa, people existed, for thousands of years. They had cultures, they had norms, they had leadership, they had everything. The Europeans came in and started changing things.

The way Africa was separated was by tribes. Each tribe has customs and beliefs. The Europeans realized they could not take one tribe and mix it with another unless they set up a system in which they could coexist without killing each other. The Europeans made compromises at times to maintain some of the existing structures, but they instituted their own systems of economics, religion, and government.

For example, Cameroon has over 53 different tribes in a country of 28 million people. How do you put all of this together to function? You set up a center of government that has a constitution and federal laws, but you maintain the chiefs for each tribe. So we ended up with a hybrid form of government and leadership.

And on the religious side, when the Europeans came, they imposed Christianity across the continent. There has been nothing like a dominant religion before. There were local beliefs, rituals, ways of living, and spirits. The Catholic religion came in and spread all over, co-existing with tribal beliefs, traditions, and customs (like it did all over the world). As with governance, Africans were allowed to maintain certain beliefs and customs. Take polygamy, for example. That's a custom that many Africans believe in. The Europeans didn't try to eliminate that, but they indoctrinated the Africans with many other aspects of their religion.

So there's a legacy of these blended cultures and belief systems, which have continued to evolve. When I was growing up, families were strongly distinguished by their religion. Mine was Catholic, and that was a focal point of our life. Now everybody's spread out, and the younger generation doesn't care much about the Church. My grandparents, if they were alive, would kill somebody for that! They were strict Catholics. I grew up in that kind of cultural environment.

At the same time, the Muslim influence from northern Africa also plays a big role in SSA. For example, the most populated country in Africa is Nigeria, and its leadership has almost always been Muslim. Unfortunately, whenever different religions and ethnicities mix, there's a tendency toward conflict. And of course when people don't have resources or opportunities to improve their lives, they often end up blaming each other. That makes the potential for conflict much higher and creates a downward spiral. So in some ways, these factors impede Africa's growth, because you have underlying potential for religious and tribal conflicts that is being fed by very difficult living conditions.

So if you're representing a business or looking for sound investment opportunities, you have to be aware of this history and these issues, especially in certain areas. Due diligence and risk assessment are essential in Africa. It's also advisable to go in with a certain degree of empathy regarding the cultural experiences (past and present) of people throughout the continent. There is a lot of complex history that has shaped African cultures as they exist today. And I contend that one of the best things Americans can do at this point is seek to understand some of this history and culture, and work with Africans to create a better future.

Cultural Themes of Sub-Saharan Africa

A great place to start is just looking at some of the basic underpinnings of SSA culture. Despite the many different cultures and traditions, it's helpful to be aware of some broader cultural tendencies across the continent. Of course, I can't give you a complete picture in one short book, but I do want to highlight a few traits for you.

Rise of Consumer Culture

One area in which Americans might be able to relate to Africans is their growing demand for a higher standard of living and better selection of consumer goods. Don't discount Africans as being poor—they are capable of spending money. Again, just look at mobile phones. Right now, down to the smallest village, people have phones. You think these people don't have any means? No, where there's a need, they will consume.

And there are plenty who do have significant financial resources. I have friends from Cameroon that come here to the US to shop and go back home, and Cameroon is not even that outstanding economically. Many Nigerians, by comparison, are quite well off these days. Africans know quality, and although cheap Chinese goods have been flooding the continent, many people hunger for better options.

And in terms of technical sophistication and the digital economy, Africans are fully embracing it. From music and arts to consumer goods to social media, more and more are joining the modern, connected world.

Respect for Elders

So that's a recent trend, but what about traditional values? In Africa, you respect your elders and speak with deference. That touches almost every single culture in Africa. You cannot have someone who's 35 years old talk down to someone who's 50, even if the younger person is the CEO and the older one is a subordinate. The culture doesn't allow that.

If somebody is your older brother or sister, you respect them til the day you die. Wealth doesn't matter. One person in a family might have all the money, while his brothers and sisters are all living a simple life in the village. When he goes to visit, he cannot sit on a chair if his penniless elder brother doesn't have a seat for himself. That would never happen.

Knowing this will help you deal with Africans. It's an important factor to think about in hiring and negotiations. They will not appreciate it if they see that you don't respect elders. It's not about money. It's not about experience, or prestige, or credentials…it's not about anything but age.

Marriage Equals Trustworthiness

Another aspect of the culture that's almost universal is a bias toward marriage as a sign of trustworthiness. If you're single, you don't get the same respect, no matter how smart you are. There are certain positions you cannot hold if you're not married. For example, they will not often let a single, unmarried person take a leadership position like running a company where you are responsible for a lot of people.

They believe that when you're married, it shows responsibility, and if you have children, that garners even more respect (which may be one of many reasons for the rapid population growth in Africa). It shows people they can count on you: "This is somebody we can trust. This is someone who can handle responsibility." Even in the case of elders, those who are not married or don't have children have less of a voice within the community. So marriage and family are in some traditions even more important than age.

Roles of Women

Historically, Africa has not had females leading or negotiating. For most African cultures, men are dominant at home. This is an area that's complex and changing, but it still has an influence on how business is done. Say, for example, you set up a company in Africa, and you have a female director or CEO. They could face some difficulties because overall men still do not believe that a woman should be in charge of them.

I'm not saying that women cannot do well in business in Africa. They definitely can and do. Opinions on women's roles and rights vary from one area to another. It's a delicate subject, and it can be confusing, especially as the culture changes.

In some ways, Africa is ahead of the US in this matter. Think about it—we've never had a female president in the US, right? But despite the long-standing discrimination against women in Africa, there have been female presidents of numerous countries. In Liberia, for example, Ellen Sirleaf was president for 12 years, and was even elected Chair of the Economic Community of West African States (ECOWAS).

Overall, it's good to be aware of this lingering issue so you have some understanding of the cultural viewpoints you might encounter. There is still a long way to go to achieve gender equality, but the situation is changing rapidly.

Mistrust and Competition Among Africans

Africans are a mixed group, like people everywhere. Some can be generous and forthright, and with others, you have to be on your guard. In general, there is a certain sense of protectiveness people have. For example, people generally don't talk about something they're working on until it's done.

I am like this. I actually didn't want anyone to know I was working on this book. I wanted it to be a surprise. I didn't even tell close friends for a long time. In the same vein, nobody at my old job knew I was in school. I thought if I let the management know, they'd use it as an excuse to fire me. And this job was very critical for me because I had all of my benefits, and the schedule was perfect for attending school.

The company actually had a tuition reimbursement program, but I didn't utilize it. I didn't tell anyone. I just kept quiet and saw to my studies. I got my undergraduate degree, went straight into law school, and nobody knew.

Toward the end, in 2009, all my classmates were preparing for the July bar. I was worried: how could I cope with finishing school, working, *and* studying for the bar? But by April, the company I was working for decided to lay off my whole work group due to the recession, so it forced my hand.

And on the last day of work, everybody was saying goodbye. A friend asked, "So what are you going to do?" I told him, "Well, I'm preparing for the bar." He laughed and said "What bar? I'll meet you there." I said, "The Massachusetts bar."

When he finally got it, he was furious, "You mean you've been in school all this time!?" He told everyone, and oh, they were not happy. One lady said, "So you've been using us to upgrade yourself?!" I couldn't believe it, but that's exactly why I hadn't said anything.

That's an African thing—we say, "Anything good you have going on, you don't let anyone know until it's done." That's when we deliver the good news. And it applies to everything we do. So when you hear somebody sharing good news, they're not just getting started. It's done.

Why? One reason is simply that everyone tends to follow this rule, so if you start talking about a project, people expect to see the results quickly. If they don't, they start judging you: "Oh, he was lying. This guy makes up stories."

Another side of it is that Africans know, one way or another, people will try to drag you down. In some ways it goes back to an old belief that whenever you plan something, if certain people find out, they'll want to jinx it. Many such belief systems hold that people have a kind of psychic superpower that lets them wreck your plans. If someone doesn't like you, they'll make sure you don't succeed. But if you just get it done quietly, then it's too late—nobody can stop you.

This might sound like superstition, but it's not so different from American or Western culture. It's pretty common that when you try to change or grow in some way, the people around you try to hold you back—they discourage you, tell you you're crazy, or do underhanded things to try to stop you. Whether it's supernatural powers or human nature or both, this is a common human experience. For Africans, we've just decided the best approach is to keep your mouth shut and do what you have to do. If somebody is starting a business, you will never have a clue until that business is up and running. Those are the dynamics that you often have to face when you're dealing with Africans. Everything is secret until it's ripe and ready. Then people are going to know.

This can make it difficult to collaborate—you really have to work to build strong relationships so people trust you. I learned this the hard way in my early days. Before I came to the US, I spent some time in South Africa. It was right after apartheid ended, and I got into a partnership with some French-speaking businesspeople from Congo who were starting up an export company. I was young, but I was useful to them because I was bilingual and had started studying the business environment there. They had connections and promised to help me get my papers so I'd be able to go to school. Once we had their company set up, they ran off and left me with nothing. And the punchline? They ended up getting scammed themselves on their first big deal and lost everything. The point is, trust is a big deal in Africa. It doesn't come easily, yet it's essential for success.

Trust: The Only Real Currency in Africa

These days, more Africans are aware of the ways in which outsiders have exploited the continent, and they're less trusting than ever. Because of colonization and the slave trade that preceded it, the experience of exploitation is long and ongoing in Africa. And even since the breakdown of the European empires in the mid 20th century, issues of political and economic control and exploitation have had a major impact on the growth and development of the continent. People are tired of not having a seat at the table for determining their own destiny, or even guiding the development of their own cultural narrative.[93]

So it's important to keep this historical context in mind when working with Africans. It's not that they're closed to working with foreigners—quite the opposite. But there is some resentment and mistrust at play as well. As mentioned in regards to corruption, people are connecting the dots that Western countries on the one hand work to fight corruption, but on the other, they enable it by helping corrupt officials hide money and remain in power.

Now you might think all of these sound like reasons to stay away, but I would argue they are reasons to get involved and change the old story for a better global future. You need to go in with eyes open about some of the issues and criticisms Africans have about outsiders.

History of Colonization

Africa started being influenced and then dominated by Europeans going back hundreds of years through the slave trade and natural resource exploitation. But the big scramble of colonization was relatively recent, shifting into high gear in the late 1800's. By the turn of the century, most of the continent was controlled by a handful of European countries. England and France were the most dominant, with Germany, Portugal, Belgium, Italy, and Spain also in the mix.

This process broke down both established kingdoms and empires as well as decentralized tribal societies. And it replaced them with new, foreign systems of societal structuring and governance, which modern countries and regions still struggle to reconcile today. The legacy of this experience can be seen in the very instability, conflict, and corruption for which the West often criticizes Africa.

Neo-Colonialism

It's widely recognized that colonization did not end with political independence for African countries. Many Africans look at Western influence of the more recent past—and even the present—as a major contributing factor to the ongoing development challenges across SSA.

Many have criticized the neoliberal economic policies imposed by Western powers, especially through the International Monetary Fund and World Bank. And not just Africans—academics, activists, and political commentators from all corners have for years pointed out the damage caused by these policies. In 2018, peasant organizations from around the world gathered in Bali and produced a unanimous condemnation of both organizations for contributing to poverty and environmental degradation.[94] Looking further back, a scathing 2012 report in *Forbes* described the World Bank as a dysfunctional mass of petty internal fiefdoms used for the personal gain of managers and their associates.[95] It cited a couple of billion dollars of missing money and annual losses in the hundreds of millions. And going further back, in 2005, a Wharton School academic report linked the two organizations with failed infrastructure projects.[96] This has always blown my mind in Africa—why would you loan money over and over for these projects and never make sure they are getting done? Whatever the reason, Africans have lost faith in these organizations, and as a consequence their trust of the West in general has further eroded.

The French Connection

Then there are political situations that crop up which enrage Africans, who feel Europeans are still tampering in their affairs. With many African countries, you might blame the leadership for certain problems, but they are beholden to the Europeans, especially the Francophone countries in SSA. France has never let go of its former colonies—any of the leaders that were against France were overthrown.

The English had a looser system in Africa, and they essentially left their colonies after independence. Not the French. They have been manipulating all these countries—the influence of France is holding back progress and keeping corrupt leaders in power to the detriment of the people, and Africans know it.

As an example, in 2019 a story came out about the firing of Arikana Chihombori-Quao, the African Union ambassador to the US. Many believed that the French were behind it, because she had given a very powerful speech against their influence in Africa.[97]

Former Ghanaian president Jerry John Rawlings was one of many who condemned the move, posting on Twitter: "The dismissal of Arikana Chihombori-Quao, AU Ambassador to the United States raises serious questions about the independence of the AU." He continued, "For someone who spoke her mind about the detrimental effects of the colonisation and the huge cost of French control in several parts of Africa, this is an act that can be best described as coming from French-controlled colonised minds. How can this shameful behaviour emanate from us? A woman with all that it takes to galvanise our continent is chopped down by French colonised power mongers good enough to be cleaners or pruning trees at the Elysée Palace. With leaders of this kind, how can this continent ever progress?"[98]

Mixed Feelings about China

These are some of the issues that comprise the background in which China has entered Africa in recent years claiming friendship: "See? The Westerners have treated you badly, but we didn't do any of that. We're here to help." But many Africans feel that the Chinese are now doing the same things or worse, making bad deals with corrupt leaders and extracting resources without benefiting the people. Opinions are mixed, but animosity is growing in many places.

Take Zambia, where as I discussed in the introduction, two riots ensued in late 2018 against Chinese nationals and their businesses. This was over allegations that the Chinese were stealing resources or taking over the country. Zambia is a country whose relationship with China goes back further than almost any other in Africa. Unfortunately, it's the working-class Chinese that take the brunt of these events, even though they themselves might not be in favor of the big state-run operations that get people afraid and upset.

On the other hand, there are those who offer counter-criticism against the West, saying their condemnation of China is simply due to a fear of losing control in the region.[99] The truth is usually somewhere in the middle, or a mix of positive and negative. No country or organization is all good or all bad, but now more than ever, the world needs the best people in every country to come out and work in good faith to build trust and create real benefit for all.

The US Needs to Protect Its Reputation and Work to Build Trust

So what about the US? As I've said, there is an overall positive feeling in Africa about the US and all things American. Isabella Erawoc, the UN logistics officer quoted in Chapter 3, weighed in on the context: "Under the Obama era," she said, "Africa was very interested in new perspectives from America. President Obama's speech in Accra in 2009 was interpreted as a counter-speech to the insulting remarks from French President Sarcozy in Dakar in 2007... There is still a certain attraction for America marked in world culture, and Africa is no exception."

However, with the focus of the past two decades on security rather than development, some of this enthusiasm has waned. And the criticisms of the World Bank and IMF also reflect poorly on America, which holds significant influence in these organizations.

Another big issue is the sheltering of money from corrupt officials in US banks and property holdings, not to mention the direct role many multinationals play in depriving developing countries of much needed funds.[100] The US also has to address its political support of corrupt politicians and rigged elections. For example, in Congo in 2019, the US State Department gave official recognition to the declared winner of the Congolese presidential election, despite the widespread view that the election had been fraudulent.[101] The reasoning was allegedly to avert further conflict in the country, but the result is that the corrupt regime continues, just in the guise of a new individual.

Unfortunately this kind of decision undermines US credibility in Africa and weakens possible business and development relations. Significant changes are needed to build trust with SSA countries and people.

Key to Success: Make Sure the People Benefit

At a broad level, it's important to show Africans that you are there for them, not just for yourself, or to impose your own culture or brand. For example, going back to the earlier discussion of tourism, I would suggest not focusing on proliferating Western hotel brands throughout Africa. Setting up African brands would be more welcomed and less likely to be viewed as either competition or only for foreigners.

You could have a chain, but you could build it through partnerships, either buying into an African brand or helping develop one. You need to be seen as coming in to develop things that are for the people, not just to take resources and make money. The "take" is the issue.

Deal with Locals

The best way to show people you're really there to create win-wins is by taking the time to understand and work with the locals. You cannot just deal with government officials; you have to deal with the people living where you want to operate. And you have to do it on their terms if you want to get anywhere. If you just go in with your contracts without understanding the customs and beliefs, there's bound to be a conflict. You have to know the culture. Without the culture you're wasting your time.

What most businesses do is sign agreements with the central government. When the government says yes, the business leaders in charge of the deal think they're all set to do what they want. But the business operations will probably not be happening at the President's house—it's going to be in some village. You have to deal with the people in the area where the resource exists. They believe that's a gift from their ancestors, right?

But you're coming in and taking it, and they're not seeing any benefits. What do you think it's going to happen? They're going to fight back.

A perfect example is the Delta region in Nigeria. This country is the number one supplier of oil in Africa and in the top 20 of the world.[102][103] Most of the oil comes from the Delta region in the south. But none of their people has access to oil. None of them own oil companies. The owners are in the north, or in other countries. As analyst Angela Ajodo-Adebanjoko wrote for Accord.org, "The region is a tale of poverty, squalor and gross underdevelopment in the midst of plenty, due to environmental degradation which has affected the people's agricultural means of livelihood. The effect of oil spills and gas flares has been death to aquatic lives and waste to farm lands."[104]

My point is not to take sides. The fact is that this conflict has been raging on and off for decades now. If we want peace and stability, we have to approach development differently, in a way that recognizes and respects both the overall culture and the subculture at the point of operation.

In Nigeria, major groups include the Hausa, the Igbo, the Ijaw Delta region people, and the Yoruba. The country also contains many smaller ethnic groups. These are distinct cultures within the same country. In fact there are over 500 languages spoken in Nigeria alone.[105] Each group has its unique cultural attributes. You cannot deal with the Hausa the same as you do with the Yoruba—that would be a big mistake.

If the people realize you're bringing something that is benefiting them, they'll protect it instead of fighting against it. Take agriculture for example. If you want to have a large farming operation, where do you get that land? It's situated in some village that's owned by some tribe. You could go to the government and have them sign off that land for you to lease for 10 or 20 years. What about the occupants of that area? You're going to have to deal with them.

You must know who you're dealing with directly. In their culture, how do they operate? If I'm going to be situated somewhere around Lagos, working with Yoruba people, I want to meet the stakeholders. I want to find out, if we want to grow a business here, what do they need (whether it's from the government or the investors) to make it successful and beneficial for them? Investing in places is not just about profit, it's about helping the people who are there and creating mutual benefit.

That all stems from the culture—what's of benefit to a particular culture may not be the same in another culture. Some might want schools, while others might want a new mosque. If that's what's good for them, that's what you want to do. Find a way—part of your contract should address that.

But the tricky thing is, it might not be obvious what they want. You need to be able to read between the lines, and that's something that takes time and experience to learn. So you need an insider.

Get Insider Connections

You need someone who's an African, who knows that even though you have to deal with the government, you have to be very aware of where your operation is going to exist. Who are the original occupants of that area?

If you have advisors that know the people, they'll guide you through the cultural terrain. So if you want to set up a new business entity, they'll know how to get the licenses, or how to negotiate to get the services and permissions you need. And they'll tell you, "Look, before we sign this deal, this is what we're going to need to do for the people of this area. This is how they operate. This is how they do business."

It's like going to someone else's home—there are conditions you have to meet in order to enter. And while some doors are open and known, most of them are hidden. That's where you need someone who knows the game, who can communicate and see what they want without them having to spell it out. For the people of Africa, just the fact that they have one of their own in front of them changes everything. Now they are free to decide, "I will agree to speak to this guy, because he will understand."

What the African people are longing for is someone sitting across from them who understands them, who looks like them, who speaks their cultural language. That's the biggest issue that Africans are facing in business dealings. With many US companies, they never see one black person, let alone someone who's from their own backyard. When they see only white people across from them, they do not feel free or open. So it's always best to seek out a diligent, trustworthy African partner who can bridge the gap between these two worlds.

Conclusion

The keys to success in Africa are focusing on win-wins, knowing the over-all culture and most importantly, the particular culture that exists where you want to do business. It's also essential to have people you trust who are insiders to these cultures. This concludes section two. We've looked at some of the challenges (both perceived and real) of doing business in Africa, as well as some of the inherent opportunities and some possible solutions. In the next section, we'll delve more deeply into best practices for success.

Solutions for Success

So far, we've looked at the unprecedented opportunity in Africa for business growth, some of the major challenges, and ways to address those challenges. In this final section, we'll expand on the solutions and explore the best practices for success in Africa.

First, we'll look at what due diligence means in the African context, a business environment that operates differently than what most Americans are accustomed to. It's essential that you understand this environment, both at the macro and the micro levels. Having experienced people on your team who can help you navigate the terrain can speed things up and pave the way for mutually beneficial relationships with local communities.

Next, we'll explore the issue of protecting your bottom line. Ensuring your revenue stream for operations in Africa isn't always as clear cut as it is in more developed countries. There is a perception that Africa is very risky, and while there are good historical reasons for that view, there are also many ways to protect your business. Recent changes in US foreign policy have opened up many exciting resources and opportunities, and we'll consider various principles and strategies.

Finally, we'll take a closer look at how doing good can ensure buy-in from locals, consumers, and investors, paving the way for long-term success. There are many benefits of focusing on social and economic development and environmental sustainability in addition to the financial bottom line. The business world is changing rapidly, and those who adopt a strong stance on social and environmental issues gain a distinct competitive advantage. Africa is a prime setting for such initiatives.

Let's dive in...

Chapter 7

Due Diligence for Investing in Africa

As we've seen, there are serious challenges present in Africa, so companies looking to tap into the many opportunities must understand and manage the risks associated with investing there.

For most US companies or investors, when somebody brings up investing in or expanding to Africa, the knee jerk reaction is, "Are you crazy?" That's because there are so many unknowns. Most of the continent is underdeveloped, so where do you begin? I'll be the first to admit that it's complicated, but with the right help and due diligence, you can protect yourself and make sound investments. That's why you need to have partners on the ground.

Corruption remains a large factor, as well as anti-corruption laws. Liability under the Foreign Corrupt Practices Act ("FCPA"), the UK Bribery Act, and other similar anti-corruption laws poses a great concern for companies. Other major considerations include political uncertainties, unfamiliar local/traditional laws, poor infrastructure, and inadequate sources of accurate information. Above all, the greatest risks are failing to understand the culture and customs of the people or assuming that they do business the way you do.

Companies operating in Africa also face serious but unique anti-corruption related challenges, such as cash-based economies, issues with agents, security factors, and special funding requests by officials. We'll take a look at these considerations in this chapter, and I've provided some self-assessment questions and topics at the end.

Dealing with Legal Systems in Africa

The legal systems in African countries don't function like they do in the US. Most American companies avoid litigation in Africa, for good reason. They favor mediation or arbitration, because they will never win in court. Somebody local goes to the back door, and gives the judge a little something. Judges don't make much, so it's common for them to take bribes. You don't want to count on the courts.

Any time you do have to deal with the courts, having trusted local partners is key. You need someone that actually knows what goes on, who's there on the ground and in court, making sure everything is legitimate. But finding those partners who are really trustworthy and capable is difficult. Personally, if a client of mine found that they needed litigation within a certain country, I would enlist a lawyer there that would take up the case, with my supervision, to fight on their behalf.

How to Find a Good Lawyer for the African Context

You want to have an attorney in the US. Don't just rely on an African attorney. It's not just about courtroom or negotiation experience. It's about the ethics and standards of being a member of an American bar. I am bound by that code—for anything I might do wrong, I am held responsible here in the US. My license could be taken, right?

As an American attorney, everything I'm doing is for the best interest of my client. If you engage someone in Africa, he might do a great job, but he doesn't have the same obligation. And it applies to anyone you might hire—you have to be very careful and not just go with the first person who claims they can help you. That person is there to benefit himself, and often his friends. That's how bribery comes about. If someone takes charge of a deal for you, they'll want to get it done by any means. They'll do whatever must be done, regardless of the ethics, bribery, and whatnot. That's how people survive in Africa.

If I'm representing a company from the US, my number one obligation is we don't get fined, so we're not going to break the law. Someone might want us to pay a bribe, but we're not going to do it. I have to come back home and be able to answer to my client as well as all the bars I belong to. And remember, with all the intricacies of the FCPA and other US laws, you could find yourself needing defense both in Africa and America.

Now, in terms of vetting an attorney, the first thing I want to know is what they've done in their career? Experience navigating through various courts in the US gives you a lot of points. It shows that this is somebody that knows what he's talking about. I've practiced before every court except the Supreme Court. I have that advantage. It's one thing to do contracts and business deals, but without an ability to defend yourself successfully in court, you are vulnerable.

For business, it's best to have a hybrid attorney, meaning someone who handles transactional dealings and contracts as well as litigation. You might need a specialist for different situations, but for your main attorney, you want someone who can navigate different arenas, make sure you're taken care of, and bring in the right specialists as needed.

Show Me the Money

In any deal with an African country, the first question to answer is how you'll get paid. If you expect money to follow you after the fact, you're wasting your time. I would not trust many African governments to pay me money.

I was talking with a colleague about a deal that had gone badly in a western African country, where the investors were owed several million dollars. He was well connected, with access all the way up to the president. He couldn't get the money out. Once it gets to that point, there's no magic that's going to fix the situation. It's too late.

Part of the way to protect yourself against getting into that kind of situation is to do things very above board. As we've seen, a lot of back-door deals still go on in Africa, and those are the ones most vulnerable to these kinds of losses.

Understanding Contracts in Africa

To Americans, a contract means we sign on the dotted lines, and we're done. In Africa, you cannot always do that. A supposed authority might sign off on a deal, but you'll find out later there are other interested parties that haven't been consulted. Some official gets 2% of the business, and no one consults the people from the affected region. That's a sure way to get into trouble.

So number one, identify where the business is going to be located. If you want to invest in agriculture, identify where the farm is going to be. Then find out who lives in the area and what their needs are. If you want to go in and be well-received, take the time to discover what you need to do to get them enthusiastically on board.

Watch Out for the Friends & Family Plan

When looking for professionals to get things done on the ground in Africa or facilitate deals, you'll hear a lot of empty promises. People will tell you they can provide whatever service you need. Don't take their word for it. Ask questions and push for details. They'll also say things like, "Oh I have a friend of a friend of a CEO who can help," or, "I have an 'in' with the president." Often, they don't know what they're doing, and they'll bring in more people who also don't know what they're doing. If you don't verify their capabilities, before you know it, you'll have wasted a ton of time and money.

You can't just go with whoever's convenient. You have to be careful who you speak to, because their goal is to make money—and better yet, to make it from both sides. On one side it's, "If you work with me, I can make XYZ happen." On the other side it's, "We need this much money." Meanwhile, he's ignoring the factors like legal risks.

If you have a professional, they're number one job should not be to get the job done by any means necessary. It should be protection. So you have to do your homework and make sure the people you're counting on are really looking out for you, legally and financially.

Importance of Being Earnest

On the flip side, *you* have to be honest and transparent with your partners or lawyers if you want that protection. One time I was involved in a lawsuit against a multinational corporation, and we had a solid case. We were on the verge of winning—it was essentially a done deal. The defendants knew we were on the brink of hitting a large judgment in this case, because we had gone through the pretrial, and they'd tried to get it dismissed. The judge said no way.

My colleagues were already celebrating. They were certain something was going to come out of it. But the opposing lawyers obtained some evidence that my client hadn't told me about, and it wrecked the whole case. It pains me to this day because we went through every single detail over and over. But they left out a crucial detail. If they had told me about this one issue, I could have obtained counter-evidence and still come out on top. I know because I had worked a similar case and won. But being blindsided like that, there was no time. There went a multi-million-dollar judgment down the drain.

This applies in all legal matters, but especially for everything you do in an unfamiliar and fluid environment like those you find in most African countries. The more you try to hide things or go through back doors, the greater your risk that things will not go well.

The Power of Partnerships

A great way to grow in Africa is by leveraging established local businesses, either as partners or by buying them out. In the US, we know mergers and acquisitions. So if you don't want to go through the process of starting from scratch and dealing with licenses and permits, investing in existing businesses is a great way to go.

Picking out a site and getting everything set up from nothing is serious. Why not bypass all that? See what's already established, go through their books, and make sure everything is okay. Do an evaluation, and lay out your terms: the percentage you want, the amount of money you'll put in. Explain that you'll maintain the people that are already there and the same license. Nothing changes, except that you are bringing money and expertise to help it grow. That'll be the safest and easiest way to begin, if you have people you can trust.

Another way to work with partnerships is to find local producers for your existing product so you can expand into the growing African markets. Coca Cola is a great example that has been all over the continent for a long time. I grew up drinking it—not all the time like it is now, usually just on holidays or Christmas, or sometimes after church. It was a special treat. Apart from the Catholic Church, Coca Cola has been the only thing you could find in almost every village in Africa, no matter how small. Anywhere you go in Africa, to the most remote location, if you don't find Coca Cola, it means something's wrong.

But here's the thing—Coca Cola didn't have factories in Africa. If you asked, "Where's the Coca Cola company?" as a standalone facility, you would not find it. There are local breweries that have contracts to produce drinks on behalf of Coca Cola and others. In Cameroon, the company that produces it is called Brasseries du Cameroun. They produce a variety of beverages: Coca Cola, Fanta, beers, etc. through partnerships with the brands.

Another example is SABMiller, the beer company. It grew into one of the largest brewers in Africa—and the world—by buying existing breweries, improving them and shifting them out of poor business practices. When its leaders started building new breweries, they bought second hand equipment and then developed partnerships with equipment suppliers to further the company's growth.[106]

SABMiller proliferated breweries all over the continent and made locally focused brands tailored to the people in a given region or country.

For example, after researching the popular culture in Nigeria, it developed a local beer brand called Hero, in alignment with the ethos of people feeling like the heroes of their own life adventures.[107] The visual branding drew on the symbolism and cultural sentiments of the Igbo people of eastern Nigeria. Launched in 2012, it has been one of the company's most popular products of all time.[108] These are smart companies who have used the power of partnerships and localized cultural understanding to get their products in the hands of hundreds of millions of Africans.

Evaluating Investment Opportunities and Assessing Risk

If you're an investor looking for a solid opportunity, you need to understand which countries serve your investment needs, because they all come with different challenges. A great resource for information on many countries you might consider is the federal government's collection of Country Commercial Guides, which you can find at www.trade.gov/ccg-landing-page.

Additionally, African countries themselves have been working hard to provide more support to foreign investors. Mouchili Mayoua, the infrastructure specialist mentioned earlier, pointed out that, "Many countries now have 'Investment Promotion Agencies,' which act as one-stop shops for investors, assisting with registration, taxes, and other steps to establish companies locally. Another important development taking place in Africa is the establishment of Commercial and Political Risks insurance solutions. This is an effort to promote foreign direct investment into developing countries to support their economic growth. You can find information at www.miga.org and iciec.isdb.org.

Conducting due diligence and investigating the available resources both stateside and in Africa will help you narrow down your options. You might decide, for example, that you don't want to go into a French zone or that you don't want to deal with a country where the political situation is even slightly unstable. Even though there are far fewer coups in recent years, some areas are safer than others. South Africa, for example, is long-established. There is general political stability, and industries are already established. The court system is independent. That's a fairly safe environment, just like investing in Europe. On the other hand, if you have the risk tolerance, you can sometimes get a higher return in a less stable area.

I know some might say, "We don't trust any of these places. You could set up operations, and then there could be some kind of conflict." But look at the trend. How many African countries are involved in wars in recent years? Oxford Research Group published a study in 2016 titled *The Coming Peace: Africa's Declining Conflicts*, which reported, "World Health Organization data shows an astonishing 95% decline in African conflict deaths from 2000 to 2012."[109] Africa does have a history of instability, but disruptions can happen anywhere, whether from protests (Hong Kong, US) to natural disasters (Australian fires) to deadly pandemics.

There are still regional conflicts that come up in Africa when people feel oppressed or radical groups want to spread their ideology. So you have to be aware of what is going on politically and any potential for conflict brewing under the surface. Part of your due diligence is to look at the atmosphere of a country. You can predict to some degree what might happen. And you can determine where to locate whatever you're trying to do within a given country. Put your business where there's more security. It's far less likely that anybody is going to cause trouble in areas where security is very solid.

In Cameroon, for example, no militants dared to go near the areas of Buea (my hometown), and Limbe, which is at the Atlantic coast with the oil refineries—even when there was conflict in surrounding areas. Why? Because those are major towns with adequate security. If you have a large operation that's making money and providing jobs, the government will likely set people to protect it. And making those connections is the role of whoever is taking you into the area. So yes, there are risks, but any investment has risks. That's where due diligence comes in.

More Location Considerations

There are places that are booming, like Nigeria, but the systems and institutions are still catching up. It's definitely gotten better. In the old days, there were stories about Nigerians actually selling oil wells or plantations they didn't own—in many cases they didn't even *know* who owned them.

It's gotten better, but it's a little tricky to navigate in terms of avoiding fraud and corruption. But in terms of development, its economy is bigger than South Africa's. That's largely attributed to oil and gas and population, but the political and business leaders are working on diversifying. So there's a lot of opportunity there if you know how to play the game.

Another factor to consider in many industries is manpower. Does the country have enough people with the know-how you need? Or can you develop it, like we've talked about previously? With the pace of change of modern industry and the lack of development, many countries are struggling to catch up. So you're not going to have immediate manpower, unless you want to provide training. You have to consider the cost and your capacity to do that.

Some industries do not require a lot of know-how. The agriculture sector doesn't require as much skill, even up to the secondary level of processing. But if you're going into areas like software, there's still a shortage of those kinds of skills. On the plus side, the manpower you will get is cheap compared to anywhere on the planet. And as Samasource has proven, you can grow a world-class workforce if you're willing to provide the necessary training. You can make a lot of money, provide jobs, and over time build a skilled labor force so you can grow, while giving people a better quality of life and more opportunity.

Narrowing Down Investment Options

Say you're an investor and you place yourself in a medium risk tolerance level. It won't ruin you to lose the money that you're investing, but of course, you want to have a good chance of making a decent return. It doesn't have to be a super-high return. You have $2 million to invest.

We've talked about finding countries that match your risk tolerance. What's going to be the next step? You have to find out what industry makes sense and how long you can wait on the return.

You want to invest in a market that you know is going to make you more money. For example, going back to some of our earlier examples, one industry that will never fail in Cameroon is the breweries. You're going to make money no matter what, because that's a sure thing. If people do nothing else, they drink beer.

Then you need to gauge the competition and determine how much of the market you need. Consider how you can minimize your entry costs. What opportunities are there for partnerships? Some operations might be quite large, but given the amount of investment, we could look for a smaller one to invest in.

Then you need to think about the timeframe to recoup your investment. Compared to oil and gas, most investments are more short-term, meaning between one and five years to at least break even. As I mentioned earlier, I think the best bet is something that's 1-2 years, but that's an individual decision. For some, if they can make their money back within five years, that's good business.

Whatever your investment needs and criteria are, I can almost guarantee you there are golden opportunities in Africa. You just have to know where to look and how to evaluate them.

Brand Recognition and Gauging Demand

Nowadays, a lot more people know where the brands they see are coming from, and they want the ones that are from the US. They almost always think that is superior. One caveat, there are a few items that other countries are better known for. Take wine for example. In most of SSA, people think of France and South Africa as the best wine producers. That's not to say a US brand couldn't compete, but it could be a little harder. For most items, American brands are preferred.

Cost is a factor. Although the middle class is growing, I would not yet recommend selling a luxury product in Africa, except in certain countries.

For South Africa, Nigeria to an extent, and northern Africa—yes, it's perfect. In Sub-Saharan Africa, you can count the number of people who will walk in and buy anything high-end. Let's say you're producing whiskey. Growing up, we knew that whiskey was a big deal. My grandfather kept some—you had to be very important for him to go into his little cabinet and pull out the Johnnie Walker to give you a shot. A bottle that costs $100 is high-end for Africa. Most regular people wouldn't be able to afford that. They want the high-tasting stuff, but they don't have the money.

So let's think about mass consumer goods that can be presented as special and superior while still being affordable. Sticking with the beverage theme, if you have a company that produces drinks, how costly is your product compared to what's already on the market? If you have something that's affordable, that's comparable, then you know you can easily hit everybody, and you're almost guaranteed to rival other brands. The advantage you have is bringing something that's foreign. Coke is a perfect example. Compared with the other soft drinks not made by Coke, the price is the same. The product is good. It's comparable to whatever else they have. But they have the brand name. People buy it.

One company that's done extremely well in Cameroon is Heineken. For almost everyone with a little bit of money, that's what they consume. Until recently, the company owned a stake in Brasseries du Cameroun.[110] Guinness is another example. Go to the smallest village and you're going to find Guinness, because years ago, people were led to believe it had health benefits. In fact, Cameroon is the fifth largest Guinness market in the world![111] I believe there are many other companies here that could do the same—use a US brand but set up local production and become a preferred choice for locals.

Maximize the US Clout Effect

A company coming from the US has an inherent clout that affects the reception it gets. The US has a lot of power. We might know this, but when you're in the States, you don't really see it. It's when you're outside the US that you realize how powerful this country's presence is. When doing business, you're treated differently. People will tend to be very careful and respectful of you.

Most people would rather do business with the US because they trust that it's going to be successful. It depends on the country. In some places, especially those with more corruption, people don't care whether you're from China or the US or anywhere else. But for the most part, it's very advantageous to be an American.

And the US' stature is not all about money and politics and culture. People forget that the US has been involved in raising the standard of living, developing a lot of countries in the world. That's why I say the US has credibility. Think about the Peace Corps. Just the education alone has made a huge impact. I myself was taught by a Peace Corps teacher when I was growing up. Those volunteers have gone to the smallest villages in almost every African country, teaching for free. And they carry on development projects in many areas. How many countries do that?

Working with the US Government

A great way to capitalize on the power of the American presence is to work with US government agencies that specialize in foreign investment and development. From the 1970s until recently, the Overseas Private Investment Corporation (OPIC) had been one of the biggest US funders of development projects around the world. Now it's evolved into the new International Development Finance Corporation. This new agency has double the budget, plus many other innovations that will help US investors and businesses conduct development projects in Africa and compete more easily with China.

Working with agencies like this, you can get extra protection both politically and financially, as well as resources to help ensure your initiative is successful. And sometimes when these kinds of agencies finance you, other banks become more interested in getting involved as well, because they know the money is guaranteed. It also puts the power and credibility of the US government behind you.

Another great tool for US businesses is to work with the US embassy in the country you want to operate or invest in. You want to know the business environment? You want to know which areas have the most risks? They have all of that information and much more. They know more about business in the areas they cover than most locals. You still have to go do your own legwork, or hire someone like myself, but they will give you a ton of support and guidance.

And if you register, they'll know there's a US company based there. The benefit of that is, you are covered. The protection of US citizens abroad is not just for your safety, it's for your investments too. For example, say you go to Malawi as a US citizen, and some trouble develops. There's a hotline. You call the embassy—I guarantee you within a short time they're going to help get you to safety. They take that very seriously. Another example—say you get sick. The embassy will connect you with the best hospitals, where they have established connections with people they trust.

That's when you realize the importance of the US government—when you're outside of the country. I went to the embassy in Cameroon, and there were over 500 local people in line. I came in, and right from security, I showed my passport. "Oh, welcome sir, welcome," and they ushered me right in. They have a lounge where you just sit and relax. They come and meet you, asking "How can we help you?" So as a citizen, you get special treatment. You don't wait in line, you just go straight in.

So there are multiple layers of personal and business protection that come from working with these various components of the American government. And if you're doing things in a clean and ethical way, as I strongly recommend, there is zero reason not to utilize these resources.

Conduct Due Diligence

Let's recap the key points from this chapter:

- Do things legitimately so you avoid fines and possible losses.
- Avoid getting in a bad situation without the US government behind you. You have a great advantage as a US citizen—use it.

- Don't assume that you can just sign a contract and expect it to be honored by the entire system. It's up to you to make sure all interested parties are considered and included.

- Institutions and systems in Africa are developing, but they're not very robust in many places yet. So you need to know how to work the system in a legitimate way, but also one that ensures you get something from your investment.

- Have a partner who knows the terrain. In terms of legal counsel, find a US-based attorney who knows both systems and can set things up in a good way to ensure you're protected.

Lastly, have a secure way to get paid. This is such a fundamental topic, it gets its own chapter, which is next.

Due Diligence Exercise

Here are a few basic questions to guide your thinking when considering investing in Africa.

1. What kind of business or industry is your company involved in or interested in?
2. What country or countries are you willing to invest in?
3. How much money are you willing to invest?
4. Are you open to mergers, acquisitions, joint ventures, or partnerships, or want to go it alone?
5. What are your investment goals, short- or long-term?
6. What is your tolerance level for uncertainties?

Once you identify those fundamentals, you need to get into more of the details. Here are the top 12 areas to consider. For each, I suggest you write down 1) what you know, 2) what you know that you don't know, and 3) anyone you can contact for additional insight (to discover factors you don't even know that you don't know).

1. Pre-entry due diligence analysis including registration and type of business formation, such as joint venture, private-private equity, private-public equity, etc.

2. On the ground compliance and due diligence procedures of local and US laws

3. Ethics and compliance matters involving the Foreign Corrupt Practices Act (FCPA), the UK bribery Act, related anti-corruption laws and various international trade laws

4. Contractual issues, including compliance vulnerabilities and risk in the countries of operation

5. Management and execution of compliance integration efforts protecting your corporation and its stakeholders

6. Human resource due diligence

7. Supply chain due diligence

8. Site selection

9. Management and execution of compliance due-diligence procedures relating to proposed third-party intermediaries, mergers and acquisitions, and joint ventures

10. Develop, conduct, and supervise training on compliance policies and procedures

11. Internal compliance investigations and audits

12. Monitor external developments, including laws and regulations, government investigations and industry best practices

Chapter 8

How to Secure Your Investment

Once you get wise to what's going on in Africa (maybe because you're reading this book) the question becomes, if you want to enter these markets, how do you ensure you'll receive the payment you're expecting? The business opportunity is there, but it must be paired with financial security.

For any business investment in Africa, it's essential that you have a reliable way to get paid. Sounds like a no-brainer, right? Everybody knows that development projects are needed, but no business is going into Africa if there's no way of ensuring a return. You have to protect yourself as you take on this kind of project.

It's a big concern. And I think that for many US companies and investors who do not know anything about Africa, it's a question they cannot answer. And it's the one that stops them from considering jumping on the many available opportunities.

You can't always count on African governments, or individuals, to come through, especially if you're on your own. Whereas in a developed economy, you might expect to have a contract where you get a percentage of payment up front and the rest on completion, in Africa, the rest might never come. Contracts aren't the be-all-end-all standard of protection that they are in the States, so you need other strategies to secure a return.

Some of the keys to success can include developing trustworthy partnerships, working with legitimate financial institutions, and getting some level of backing from the US government. This chapter will present several options that provide exciting opportunities for US businesses looking to invest in developing Africa to do so with confidence they'll be paid.

Understanding the Business Environment

Any company that's going to invest its time, energy, and resources needs to make money. But in most SSA countries, the governments are not very reliable—you can't always depend on them to pay you. Many of them have issues with corruption, or they're facing economic problems like out-of-control debt.

At the same time, independent organizations and individuals you might rely on as partners or allies can turn out to be looking for opportunities to short-change you. There's a lack of presumed trust across the continent, meaning you really have to work at it. Until trust has been established, many people will tend to look after themselves and maximize any opportunity for gain, even at others' expense.

It is definitely possible, and even essential, to build relationships of trust with local partners, but it can take time. You either need someone who already has those relationships, or you need to be willing to play a long game, demonstrating both savvy and goodwill.

Barrett Raftery of GivePower shared his insights from over a decade of work around SSA:

"The risk tolerance is different in Africa, that's for certain. I think it's harder for Americans because it's a less contractual and more relational marketplace. Having specific knowledge of the places you work, and the network of people there that are connected and effective in those places, is particularly critical in SSA.

The lessened ability to collect via legal means creates a greater reliance on trust than ever. Make sure you have vetted your partners and spent a lot of face time with them—email and remote relationships are much harder to build and maintain. I wouldn't be effective if I didn't have a lot of relationships that have been built over many years in a specific market, and that knowledge is highly localized."

As we've explored previously, success in Africa depends largely on knowing the locale where you intend to operate or invest—the people, the culture, and the business and political environment. Another big factor is creating a safety net for yourself by partnering with US federal agencies and other reliable institutions.

Partnering with US Government Agencies

Until recently, the US was failing to counter the Chinese approach in Africa effectively, or even compete with European countries that have more robust national foreign investment policies. With Chinese investment, most of the companies are being financed by state-owned banks, which is basically the government doing it all. Meanwhile, in the West, the governments are not involved at that level. We have private investors, private entities, private banks. So it's a big difference.

But recent changes have opened major opportunities for US businesses to be able to compete and support real, meaningful development. While it's not strictly necessary to work with the government in order to be successful, the more you can involve federal agencies and get their support, the more security you'll have.

Some people go in and do deals they don't want anyone to know about—they don't want any official involvement. Usually it's because they're doing things they know they shouldn't be doing, and a lot of times those people get into trouble. When that happens, there's nothing they can do. They can't run to the embassy for help. So my argument is that it's better for all sides to do things above board, and in many cases, to get the US behind you. At any rate, you should know about the available resources so you can decide for yourself if they're worth pursuing.

There has been a major push within the US government in the last few years to reimagine America's relationship with Africa. In 2018, this push generated the launch of "Prosper Africa", a vast initiative involving more than 15 government agencies. According to the website:

> "For years companies have asked the U.S. Government to make it easier to access its trade and investment support services. Prosper Africa answers this call by providing a one-stop shop that makes the full range of those services available to U.S. and African businesses and investors. Through Prosper Africa, the U.S. Government helps to unleash the entrepreneurial spirit of Americans and the people of African nations like never before — advancing American and African prosperity and security, supporting jobs, and demonstrating the superior value of transparent markets and private enterprise for driving growth."[112]

This initiative is continuing to evolve, for example with the more recent launch of the International Development Finance Corporation (DFC). This is a great step forward for American businesses. Launched at the beginning of 2020, it merged the Overseas Private Investment Corporation (OPIC) with the US Agency for International Development's (USAID) Development Credit Authority (DCA).

It represents a significant step in ramping up American private sector investment in developing countries, with Africa considered of prime importance. It's also part of a new push to counter China's state-financed approach to development, which has gone relatively unchallenged for years.

The purpose of the DFC is to support and encourage private sector investments in underdeveloped countries.[113] It offers a variety of new finance tools previously unavailable from its predecessor agencies. One of the most important innovations of this agency is the ability to provide equity, whereas OPIC could only provide debt. And there's a lot more on offer:

> "In addition to OPIC and DCA's previous capabilities, DFC is equipped with new resources and tools to multiply its impact.

Enhancements include an investment cap of $60 billion—more than double OPIC's $29 billion limit—and new financial tools such as equity investments, technical assistance, and feasibility studies to more proactively address development needs ...

DFC will advance a private sector-led model that supports development by providing businesses with financing, insurance, and other financial tools when they are unavailable or insufficient from commercial sources. These development finance tools can mobilize significant private capital into the developing world, where government resources alone are not enough to meet pressing needs and challenges."[114]

These new capabilities are helping US companies compete more effectively with China, as well as their European counterparts.[115] If you can show that you're going to work in an emerging market and how it's helping the people, the DFC may provide the funds, and they'll be insured. The number one goal is that their projects provide real development and economic benefit. It's not just the profit, it's what that project is going to do for the people. If you look at their funding, it's generally attached to things like supplying drinking water, health care, sanitation, jobs...projects that will help the poor and contribute to the economy.

The DFC is designed to make money as well, because it has equity in whatever projects it funds. So it operates at no net cost to the American taxpayer. By having it as a funding partner, you get the force of the US government behind you to make sure that all parties uphold their ends of the deal. Just the fact that you have such a powerful entity in your corner covers you against a lot of potential problems, because nobody wants to cross the US.

Beyond financing, the DFC's involvement includes assistance with logistics and project organization. It has staff members with expertise in almost every emerging market. Consider this a primary go-to resource for planning and financing development projects in Africa.

USAID is still an independent agency that is also part of Prosper Africa, and it has some new tricks up its sleeve, in the form of its recently developed Private-Sector Engagement Policy (PSE). Like the DFC, USAID is seeking partnerships with private companies to enhance overseas development efforts.

"USAID is undertaking a major cultural and operational transformation to expand Private Sector Engagement Agency-wide. Through its new PSE Policy, USAID has issued an Agency-wide call to action and mandate to work hand-in-hand with the private sector to design and deliver our development and humanitarian programs in all sectors. This policy signals an intentional shift towards enterprise-driven development as a more sustainable way to empower people, communities and countries on their journey to self-reliance."[116]

The Export-Import Bank is yet another agency that helps with a variety of international projects, giving loans, providing credit insurance, and many other tools to help US businesses compete internationally. And it's guaranteed by the US Treasury.

For every project the US gets involved in, it will have people on the ground to make sure that it comes to fruition, one way or another. These agencies want to partner with US entities that can do the job. The US doesn't play around. It gets things done, and that's why its reputation is very high.

Every business needs profit, but more and more are doing a public service as well as making money. Those are the ones that take the risk, for example, of going into rural areas where they've never had electricity, water, healthcare, or living-wage jobs. Those kinds of projects are strong candidates for one or more of these agencies to help with, because their purpose is to be part of doing something good.

Call Your Friendly Neighborhood Embassy

For just about any dealings in Africa, I would suggest you make use of the US Embassy's business attaché. They'll make sure they're talking to the government of that country to protect the interests of US businesses. They can also provide you most of the information you actually need in a country. When you go to the embassy, you're going to get it.

If you do things properly, you'll have a contract that you know could be enforced no matter the situation. Then if they do not pay, the embassy can help you collect. The ambassador can call the president directly: "My guys are trying to help your people. They invested here, and this is what's going on..." I guarantee you there's going to be action. But it's best to have embassy staff involved beforehand if you want their help when a problem arises.

Working with Development Finance Institutions

You can also consider working with finance institutions outside of the US government. Most African countries, for example, get loans or development money from the IMF or the World Bank. We discussed these earlier, and while there are many problems, they are still go-to resources.

Other examples of credible financial institutions in Africa include the Islamic Development Bank (IDB) and the African Development Bank (ADB). As the names suggest, these banks fund development projects throughout the continent, and they are always looking for quality business partners to carry out projects.

These institutions are well-established, and companies get paid directly from the bank to fulfill the projects they fund, so it's secure. The involved country benefits, the bank makes money, and the company is paid—wins on all sides.

So how does an American company come into the picture? Unless you are known in the country, it's going to be on you to develop an outreach program. Identify which countries are best suited for you to operate in, and make yourself known to the decision makers and project coordinators in that country. As a business owner or investor, you could even be the one to initiate or suggest a project in the first place. Like any business deal—you identify your ideal prospect, develop a connection, and present a proposal. You can also hire someone to facilitate this process, find the decision makers, establish communications, and broker deals.

Then the government or local partner will have to see if they have the needed resources. If they don't have the cash, they can then turn to whichever financing institution makes sense and is willing to work with them. Whoever funds the project, it's up to them to determine that they trust that country to pay it back, and that they trust you to complete the project satisfactorily.

Funding in Africa is a strange and ever-evolving system, because many African governments are in default, and many funded projects never get completed. The money often disappears somewhere along the way. So you'd think they could not go back, for example, to the IMF or World Bank. However they still do. People don't want to admit it, but it happens. So the money is still available—it's just that more companies with the ethics and standards to see projects through are sorely needed.

Despite the flaws with these institutions, if there's a cohesive plan and it's going to provide development, they will likely support it. And if the country is getting a loan from one of them and you're getting paid directly from the institution, then you're set. Just make sure you get the job done!

Find Creative Ways to Get Paid

Let's look at a few other approaches to ensuring that you receive payment for your efforts. This is by no means a comprehensive list—the point is to help you think creatively about how you could operate successfully and profitably in the different environments of SSA.

Equity Deals

One approach to getting paid involves creating agreements to receive a percentage of revenue from the asset you develop. For example, if a government agrees, a private company could build major roads between cities and collect tolls for a certain number of years. It has to be major, because you want roads that will have high traffic, so there are enough tolls.

Ambassador Ringo arranged such a deal for power generation in Ghana using a new proprietary green technology.

"We went to them and said, 'Listen, we want to bring these units to generate electricity.' Of course, the first question they asked was, 'Okay what's it going to cost us.'

Our answer? 'Zero.' We said, 'We will manufacture the units in Ghana. We will place them on site. We will train Ghanaian people to operate them.'

So then how do we make money? Well, whenever they start producing electricity, 80% of the money generated will go to the Ghanaian government and 20% to our investors. Now, you might think 20% doesn't sound like a lot, but when you generate 100 megawatts of electricity for 20 years, that's a lot of money. And governments love it because they don't have to put out a dime."

NGOs

There are also NGOs that conduct all kinds of development projects. If you can partner with these types of organizations, they can serve as the financing institution. They raise the money and pay whoever they think is best suited to do the work or provide materials and support.

Say an NGO wants to set up a clinic in a certain area to help an underserved population that lacks access to health care. They might need to hire out various aspects of the project, and in some cases, it might make sense to bring in American experts. This will vary by industry, region, and organization, but whatever your field, you could search for NGOs that might need your skill set and find out if there's an opportunity to partner with them.

Collateral Deals

Another approach is to arrange collateral deals—building into a contract that you are entitled to some existing asset if the client is unable to pay. This will vary by country and region, so due diligence is important, researching what assets and resources they have. What do they export? What do they have that brings in revenue?

You also have to consider the potential negative impact on the country or client. How much could you recoup from that asset, if necessary, without running them bankrupt? How could you structure the deal in a way that creates more money for them than they're giving up, so the benefit outpaces the expense?

The numbers have to work out on both sides, or you could end up doing more harm than good. This is a little tricky, because on the one hand, you don't want to take the Chinese approach of debt-trap diplomacy and back-door deals to appropriate assets. But on the other hand, you want to make sure your investment is covered.

You might want to get the American government behind you on this kind of deal to make sure it will be upheld. You have to make sure it's structured according to international standards, so it's legally binding, even if the local government changes. If there is something that's internationally known and legally binding, you're going to get your money.

You're Going to Need a Plan

Financing institutions need to see a comprehensive plan. They'll want to know where the funds are going and how the project will get completed. You must have the right people in the right places, know what permits and licenses are required, and so on.

Let's use electricity as an example. In Benin, over 60% of the country has never had electricity. The only place you can find a significant amount of electricity is in the main capital. It looks like a great opportunity. If we want to take on a project to expand electricity generation and delivery, we have to calculate the size, scope, and necessary logistics. What area are we covering? How much wattage do we need to produce? How about materials? How about manpower? Do we bring in experts from the States, or are there enough local people that have the know-how? Are there aspects for which we could train locals so as to provide some upskilling as part of the project? You need all such questions answered to show a financier.

If there's an existing project or business, and you're coming in as an equity partner to improve it, that's a little different. Everything is set, and you're just going to develop and make it bigger and better. You still need to cover the logistics, but there's more to work with.

If there's a wide-open space, though, like in Benin where there's virtually no electricity infrastructure, it might not be an option to go in on an existing project. So in that case you have to start from scratch. That's when it's most critical to lay out every detail and know where the money is coming from.

Contracting with the US Government

Apart from the federal agencies mentioned earlier in this chapter, various departments in the US government have contractors handling an array of projects both domestically and internationally. Most Americans are not aware of these initiatives or how to become a contractor, but those who know the system have a lot of opportunity. With just a little research, you'll be amazed at the number and variety of opportunities.

You might be surprised that you don't have to be a large company to get government contracts. In fact, according to USA.gov, "Each year, the government awards hundreds of billions of dollars in federal contracts to businesses to meet the needs of federal agencies and the military. The government's goal is to award at least 23 percent of those contracts to small businesses."[117]

Go to https://www.usa.gov/government-contracting-for-beginners for more details. This site provides a ton of information and resources for getting set up as a government contractor, finding projects, bidding, and more.

One essential criterion is going to be that you know the environment you'll be working in and how to get things done within it. Whether you conduct your own due diligence or partner with someone like myself to speed up the process, you'll need to demonstrate your ability to navigate the local waters.

The end goal is that the US wants its money to produce results, and depending on the agency, to generate a return. That means they're going to find someone that they trust will get it done. And that's where more private companies are needed. If you can show you have the experience, the knowledge, and the support to operate in the environment and the culture, you can become a preferred partner and have a secure way to get paid for your efforts.

Conclusion

It's an exciting time for US businesses willing to open up to foreign development, and there's no better place than Africa. Most of these countries do not have a lot of money, but they have the need, and with a little ingenuity, you can find ways to do good, get paid well, and grow your business.

The main point is that you don't just go in on your own expecting a standard contract to be honored or an African government to pay you upon completion. Some will, but some of them are just dead broke. So if you see opportunities, but they don't have the funds, you have to look for other means.

We know there's potential, so get creative. Find out what financial resources exist, develop a solid plan, and see how the rest can be covered in a secure way. Millions of underserved people have a dire and urgent need for the resources and expertise America can offer. With the variety of new investment tools and initiatives now available, and the vast array of opportunities waiting throughout the continent, I urge anyone wanting to make great money and have a positive impact on the world to dive in now.

In our final chapter, we're going to spend a little more time on the positive impact piece and why it's so essential to business success in Africa.

Chapter 9

Good Business Means
Doing Good

The world of business has changed dramatically in recent years towards a more holistic view of economic and social sustainability. This transformation continues to progress rapidly in the face of the many urgent crises facing society today.

Cone Research reported that environmental, social, and governance metrics have become more important than ever to investors, with over 80% weighing these metrics in their decision-making process.[118] The same research estimated that global investments guided by these criteria were approaching $20 trillion, "a quarter of all professionally managed investments."[119]

Not only that, I would argue that in this time when everything has been disrupted by COVID-19, it's more important than ever to focus on values. How else can we use this opportunity to shape a better, more vibrant future for our world?

Africa provides one of the most fertile areas for melding business interests with the common good. It has historically been considered a treasure trove of resources to be exploited, and unfortunately there are still plenty of people who view the continent in such a predatory way. But more and more, as I hope you've seen in this book, the real opportunity is proving to be found in solving problems on the continent. This is the path to long-term growth potential and profit for individuals and companies with the heart to do good.

Giving advancement opportunities to the people who live where you operate gives you an advantage in terms of business success. In fact, it's essential. You have to build trust within the community you're working or investing in. Figure out what they need and find a way to help, whether it's building roads or clinics, establishing reliable electricity generation, or anything else.

Ambassador Ringo shared his thoughts: "Making money cannot be the number one priority for investment in Africa. The number one priority has to be, "What can I do to improve the quality of life of the people of the African continent?" ...knowing that at the end of the day, we *will* make money as a result."

Earlier I discussed the idea of setting up manufacturing at the site of natural resource production and extraction. China has already started doing this. Irene Yuan Sun, author of *The Next Factory of the World: How Chinese Investment is Reshaping Africa*, described how Chinese companies faced with rising costs at home have been increasingly outsourcing, many ending up in Africa.[120]

An excerpt featured in *Quartz Africa* shared her insight that these companies are finding success in a variety of industries, not only in export-based businesses, but also in domestic African markets like Nigeria.[121]

But she acknowledged that some of these companies are lacking in the ethics needed for truly sustainable development, citing racism, bribery, and poor (or even dangerous) treatment of African workers. Africa needs a higher ethical standard for this industrialization.

And what about infrastructure that actually benefits locals? The companies extracting minerals have constructed some of the best roads in these regions, for example, but it's only for themselves. Their roads make it easier for them to take the material away. What if someone with a little more humanity went in and did more? What if you developed the essential infrastructure to allow the people there a decent life? Who would they rather do business with?

Even if infrastructure is not your area of expertise, as an American, you have resources at your disposal that could help get these things done. Those resources are beyond anything many African communities can imagine. And if you're willing to tap into them, the goodwill you can generate with the people will lay the foundation for long-term growth and stability. The wisest approach is to find ways to satisfy people's needs in the areas where natural resources come from. Go in with the intention to improve and create.

There are two missions: make profit, and do it by uplifting the lives of the people. So if, for example, cobalt is coming from a particular village, see that it becomes one of the most beautiful villages imaginable. People don't need much for a decent life: schools, roads, water, electricity. That is easy. And when it's done, it's done. All that's needed then is maintenance and upgrades over time, which can be delegated to the people once they're empowered with the means and the knowledge.

If you take care of the area in which you operate, you can be there for as long as you want. People back home will wonder how you could manage in such a supposedly volatile area without conflict. And they'll come to realize it's because you went in not looking just at the bottom line, but at building relationships and being of service. That's exciting for both consumers and investors these days, and they'll be more likely to support your business.

Being fair and being good is good business for you. Maybe you won't have quite the level of short-term profit that you could by going through back doors. However, your risk will be much lower, and your business more sustainable, because people will want you there. They'll want to be part of what you're doing. So if you take a long view, it's much more profitable. And as I pointed out early on, we are all connected, so why not work to create a better world for everyone, and make your money from that?

I think most Americans have the motivation and the morals to be the ethical leaders in business. No company wants to be linked with child labor, sweat shops, or abusive working conditions. But I believe it's time for American companies to go beyond trying to avoid the worst situations, and start proactively creating the best.

Do More Good

Some companies are really taking a stand and providing opportunities for the African people. General Electric is a great example of a large company that has truly invested in Africa for the long haul. One way they've been helping is by providing training and education in the areas of science, technology, and business.

Former President and CEO of GE Africa Jay Ireland told representatives from McKinsey &Co. in 2019 that his team had recognized early on the crucial role of talent development in Africa. To address this need, they brought all of GE's management training programs to Africa, and enlisted hundreds of recent graduates. Those trainees have gone on to become the next generation of leaders for the company.[122]

And GE is not the only one working to fill the education gap. Recall Samasource, for example, the technology company that grew from nothing and has now trained thousands of tech professionals and become a global leader in machine learning (a.k.a. artificial intelligence). McKinsey researchers have concluded in the last couple of years that Africa is at the beginning of a "corporate education revolution." Its research showed that over 60% of the top-performing companies on the continent run such programs.[123]

GE has also been a major player in infrastructure development with a long history on the continent. Their Sub-Saharan Africa web page states:

"GE works on things that matter; the best people with the best technology tackling the world's toughest challenges. In Sub-Saharan Africa, GE is helping to build, cure, move and power the region for a sustainable future. GE has been in Sub-Saharan Africa for over 100 years, demonstrating its commitment to the region through energy solutions, medical equipment, transportation, finance and infrastructure."[124]

One major branch of GE's operations is in renewable energy. In 2019, for example, it launched a new initiative to provide and upgrade power in West Africa, to both Benin and Cote d'Ivoire. Globally, it has installed more than 400+ gigawatts of clean renewable energy and employs nearly 40,000 people in more than 80 countries. The company's philosophy is clear:

"GE Renewable Energy is a $15 billion business which combines one of the broadest portfolios in the renewable energy industry to provide end-to-end solutions for our customers demanding reliable and affordable green power...GE Renewable Energy creates value for customers seeking to power the world with affordable, reliable and sustainable green electrons."[125]

Small Organizations Can Make a Big Difference Too

Now, GE is a large company with vast resources at its disposal, but you don't have to be a megacorp to do great work that uplifts people and brings you profit and growth. Think about Beyond Good, the chocolate company discussed earlier. Although tiny compared to GE, it has been able to make a meaningful impact on the lives of hundreds of cocoa farmers, provide jobs, as well as support infrastructure projects and environmental protection.

The company's website expresses its values: "...We're working towards a world where farmers make good money. A world where farmers are not a statistic. A world where farmers are treated like people, and not photo ops."[126]

Although local production has provided challenges, the company's success, and the success of workers earning a livelihood in humane conditions speaks volumes.

"The typical chocolate supply chain usually has anywhere from 3-5 middlemen sitting between the cocoa farmer and the chocolate maker. That doesn't work for farmers and it doesn't work for us...Zero middlemen means 100% transparency and farmers make 6X the industry standard."[127] Inefficient and exploitive industries are ripe for disruption, and innovative companies like this can profit in the process.

Nonprofits too can make a big difference. Charity: Water is a great example of a grassroots organization that has grown to a large scale by empowering and funding locally-driven water projects in underdeveloped areas in Africa and around the world. GivePower Foundation, mentioned earlier, has also done a tremendous job changing lives in just a few short years. Its solar energy systems have powered food production and clean water. They've also provided electricity for schools, businesses, and emergency services. The organization has assisted with animal and land conservation efforts as well. At the time of writing, its website reported, "We've powered over 2,650 schools across 17 countries and changed the lives of over 400,000 people."[128]

Whether you start a nonprofit, partner with one, or look to them for inspiration, there is a lot for investors and the business community to gain and learn from the nonprofit world.

These are just a few examples of businesses and organizations leading the way in Africa, modeling the financial and social benefits of operating in a sustainable, ethical way. The win-win development model is here to stay and is imperative for long-term success in Africa. As Ambassador Ringo put it, "The key in building a strong Africa is to empower from within. Africa has the resources, the passion, and the ability of the people. They just need the proper opportunities to develop and grow their countries."

Closing Thoughts

In 2019 I reached 10 years of law practice. It's been good in the sense of winning trials, but to me, the actual trial is secondary. What matters most is preparing the case.

You have to be on your game. And I always felt I had to put in double the effort, because of who I am, being an African and having an accent. So I've always worked to up my game to the point where the other side can have no doubt this guy knows what he's talking about.

The judge also knows when you're prepared and when you're not. Some will insult you—I've seen it happen, and I vowed never to be in that position. When they see you are doing a good job, they appreciate it, and they encourage you to achieve even more.

This holds true in the business world too, especially in Africa. People there have seen it all, and they smell deception a mile away. You have to be on your game. And you also have to be savvy—know the terrain, and know what you can bring to the table to add value. Then you have to bring it.

I love it here in America. I've gotten a lot of support (and worked very hard to earn it), and I see my experience as a microcosm of how the US can help Africa. From my former officemates in Boston to the professors, colleagues, and judges who have encouraged me and opened up doorways, it's been amazing. And now I want to return the favor by opening up doors in Africa for you.

How Africa develops in the next decade will shape the direction of humanity, and the planet, for many decades to come. All signs point to the continent being by far the largest percentage of the world's population and its biggest economic driver.

Yet its development comes at a critical time when the ecological future of the planet hangs in the balance. Therefore it's critical for the long-term well-being of our species that Africa develops in a sustainable way. The US is the perfect partner to make that happen.

I hope you've found this book inspiring, and if you're interested in getting involved, I invite you to get in touch so we can explore the best options in Africa for you.

Get In Touch

info@AfricanLegalConcierge.com

508-612-7490

AfricanLegalConcierge.com

Notes

Introduction

1. Damian Hattingh, Acha Leke, and Bill Russo, "Lions (still) on the move: Growth in Africa's consumer sector, McKinsey & Company, October 2, 2017 https://www.mckinsey.com/industries/consumer-packaged-goods/our-insights/lions-still-on-the-move-growth-in-africas-consumer-sector

2. "Population," United Nations, cited May 10, 2020 https://www.un.org/en/sections/issues-depth/population/index.html

3. https://www.hoover.org/research/africa-2050-demographic-truth-and-consequences

4. Jake Bright and Aubrey Hruby, *The Next Africa*, Thomas Dunne Books: St. Martin's Press, New York, p122

5. Al Jazeera, "Mapping Africa's natural resources: An overview of the continent's main natural resources," *Al Jazeera*, February 20, 2018 https://www.aljazeera.com/indepth/interactive/2016/10/mapping-africa-natural-resources-161020075811145.html

6. Makhtar Diop, "Foresight Africa 2016: Banking on agriculture for Africa's future," *The Brookings Institution*, January 22, 2016 https://www.brookings.edu/blog/africa-in-focus/2016/01/22/foresight-africa-2016-banking-on-agriculture-for-africas-future/

7. Abdur Rahman Alfa Shaban, "Why is Africa importing $35bn in food annually? - AfDB boss asks," *Africanews*, Last updated: April 21, 2017. https://www.africanews.com/2017/04/21/why-is-africa-importing-35bn-in-food-annually-afdb-boss-asks//

8. Aubrey Hruby, "Deconstructing the Dragon: China's Commercial Evolution in Africa," *The Atlantic Council*, July 11, 2019, p2 https://issuu.com/atlanticcouncil/docs/deconstructing_the_dragon-china_s_c

Chapter 1

9. Kingsley Ighobor, Aissata Haidara, "All eyes on $1 trillion: African agribusiness is set for a huge leap, according to a World Bank report," *United Nations Africa Renewal, Special Edition on Agriculture 2014* https://www.un.org/africarenewal/magazine/special-edition-agriculture-2014/all-eyes-1-trillion

10. Makhtar Diop, "Foresight Africa 2016: Banking on agriculture for Africa's future," *Brookings Institution*, January 22, 2016 https://www.brookings.edu/blog/africa-in-focus/2016/01/22/foresight-africa-2016-banking-on-agriculture-for-africas-future/

11. David Reese, "African Immigrants Doing Well in United States," *Courthouse News Service*, December 14, 2017 https://www.courthousenews.com/african-immigrants-doing-well-in-united-states/

12. Megan French Dunbar, "Social Entrepreneur Leila Janah is Using Online Work to Fight Poverty," *Conscious Company Media*, March 5, 2016 https://consciouscompanymedia.com/sustainable-business/social-entrepreneur-leila-janah-is-using-online-work-to-fight-poverty/

13. "Central African Economic and Monetary Community," *International Democracy Watch*, cited May 11, 2020 http://www.internationaldemocracywatch.org/index.php/central-african-economic-and-monetary-community

14. Boureima Balima, "How Africa's free-trade zone will provide an economic boom," *World Economic Forum* (in collaboration with *Reuters*), July 8, 2019 https://www.weforum.org/agenda/2019/07/africas-free-trade-zone-economic-boom

15. MacDonald Dzirutwe,"Mugabe's farm seizures: racial justice or catastrophic power grab?" *Independent*, September 6, 2019 https://www.independent.co.uk/news/world/africa/robert-mugabe-death-zimbabwe-land-reform-white-farm-seizures-a9094511.html

16. "Zimbabwe abandons its currency," *BBC*, last updated January 29, 2009 http://news.bbc.co.uk/2/hi/7859033.stm

17. "Climate Action Summit 2019 Closing Release," *United Nations*, September 23, 2019 https://www.un.org/en/climatechange/assets/pdf/CAS_closing_release.pdf

18. Luke Daniel, "A look at China's big plans for Limpopo and why locals should be concerned," *The South African*, September 12, 2018 https://www.thesouthafrican.com/news/china-south-africa-limpopo-coal-concern/

19. "Business Roundtable Redefines the Purpose of a Corporation to Promote 'An Economy That Serves All Americans'," *Business Roundtable*, August 19, 2019   https://www.businessroundtable.org/business-roundtable-redefines-the-purpose-of-a-corporation-to-promote-an-economy-that-serves-all-americans

20. "Our Commitment," *Business Roundtable*, Cited May 11, 2020 https://opportunity.businessroundtable.org/ourcommitment/

21. Irene Yuan Sun, "Africa will take China's place as the next factory of the world," *Quartz Africa*, November 6, 2017 https://qz.com/africa/1120730/africa-will-be-the-next-factory-of-the-world/

Chapter 2

22. Neo Sisinye, "66 percent of sub-Saharan Africans are listed as "unbanked" – World Bank," *IT News Africa*, December 7, 2018, "https://www.itnewsafrica.com/2018/12/66-percent-of-sub-saharan-africans-are-listed-as-unbanked-world-bank/

23. Roxana Elliott, "Mobile Phone Penetration Throughout Sub-Saharan Africa, *GeoPoll*, July 8, 2019, https://www.geopoll.com/blog/mobile-phone-penetration-africa/

24. Press Release: "Financial Inclusion on the Rise, But Gaps Remain, Global Findex Database Shows," *The World Bank*, April 19, 2018, https://www.worldbank.org/en/news/press-release/2018/04/19/financial-inclusion-on-the-rise-but-gaps-remain-global-findex-database-shows

25. Killian Fox, "Africa's mobile economic revolution," *The Guardian*, July 23, 2011, https://www.theguardian.com/technology/2011/jul/24/mobile-phones-africa-microfinance-farming

26. Elliot Smith, "The US-China trade rivalry is underway in Africa, and Washington is playing catch-up," CNBC, October 9, 2019, https://www.cnbc.com/2019/10/09/the-us-china-trade-rivalry-is-underway-in-africa.html

27. Mailyn Fidler, "African Union Bugged by China: Cyber Espionage as Evidence of Strategic Shifts," *Council on Foreign Relations*, March 7, 2018, https://www.cfr.org/blog/african-union-bugged-china-cyber-espionage-evidence-strategic-shifts

28. Haisam Hassanein, "Arab States Give China a Pass on Uyghur Crackdown," *The Washington Institute*, August 26, 2019, https://www.washingtoninstitute.org/policy-analysis/view/arab-states-give-china-a-pass-on-uyghur-crackdown

29. Jenni Marsh, "Free gift? China extends influence in Africa with $32M grant for regional HQ," *CNN*, March 30, 2018 https://www.cnn.com/2018/03/27/asia/ecowas-china-headquarters-intl/index.html

30. Joan Tilouine and Ghalia Kadiri, "A Addis-Abeba, le siège de l'Union africaine espionné par Pékin," *Le Monde*, January 27, 2018https://www.lemonde.fr/afrique/article/2018/01/26/a-addis-abeba-le-siege-de-l-union-africaine-espionne-par-les-chinois_5247521_3212.html

31. Abdi Latif Dahir, "China "gifted" the African Union a headquarters building and then allegedly bugged it for state secrets," *Quartz Africa*, January 30, 2018 https://qz.com/africa/1192493/china-spied-on-african-union-headquarters-for-five-years/

32. John Aglionby, Emily Feng, Yuan Yang, "African Union accuses China of hacking headquarters," *Financial Times*, January 29, 2018 https://www.ft.com/content/c26a9214-04f2-11e8-9650-9c0ad2d7c5b5

33. Nick Van Mead, "China in Africa: win-win development, or a new colonialism?" *The Guardian*, July 31, 2018, https://www.theguardian.com/cities/2018/jul/31/china-in-africa-win-win-development-or-a-new-colonialism

34. Jonathan W. Rosen, "'China Must Be Stopped': Zambia Debates the Threat of Debt-Trap Diplomacy," *World Politics Review*, December 18, 2018 https://www.worldpoliticsreview.com/insights/27027/china-must-be-stopped-zambia-debates-the-threat-of-debt-trap-diplomacy

35. Aglionby, Feng, Yang, *Financial Times*https://www.ft.com/content/c26a9214-04f2-11e8-9650-9c0ad2d7c5b5

36. John Hursh, "Tanzania Pushes Back on Chinese Port Project," *The Maritime Executive*, December 2, 2019, https://www.maritime-executive.com/editorials/tanzania-pushes-back-on-chinese-port-project

37. Rosen, "'China Must Be Stopped'..."

38. Fidler, *Council on Foreign Relations* https://www.cfr.org/blog/african-union-bugged-china-cyber-espionage-evidence-strategic-shifts

39. Nicole Gaouette and David McKenzie, "African Union, African UN envoys demand Trump apology," *CNN*, January 13, 2018 https://www.cnn.com/2018/01/12/politics/african-union-demands-trump-apology/index.html

40. "Prosper Africa," International Trade Administration, cited July 31, 2020 https://www.trade.gov/prosper-africa

41. Danielle Paquette, "Trump administration unveils its new Africa strateg, — with wins and snags," *The Washington Post*, June 19, 2019 https://www.washingtonpost.com/world/trump-administration-unveils-its-new-africa-strategy--with-wins-and-snags/2019/06/19/c751be4c-91f5-11e9-956a-88c291ab5c38_story.html?noredirect=on

42. "Suspected Boko Haram suicide bombers kill several in northern Cameroon," *France 24*, April 6, 2020, https://www.france24.com/en/20200406-suicide-bombers-kill-several-in-northern-cameroon-boko-haram

43. "Cameroon: Victims of Boko Haram attacks feel abandoned in the Far North," *Amnesty International*, December 11, 2019, https://www.amnesty.org/en/latest/news/2019/12/cameroon-victims-of-boko-haram-attacks-feel-abandoned-in-the-far-north/

44. Helene Cooper, "Boko Haram and ISIS Are Collaborating More, U.S. Military Says," *The New York Times*, April 20, 2016, https://www.nytimes.com/2016/04/21/world/africa/boko-haram-and-isis-are-collaborating-more-us-military-says.html

45. Katrina vanden Heuvel, "America's expanding 'shadow war' in Africa," *The Washington Post*, November 1, 2017, https://www.washingtonpost.com/opinions/americas-expanding-shadow-war-in-africa/2017/11/01/a24d68ee-bdbc-11e7-8444-a0d4f04b89eb_story.html

46. Cara Anna, "Why US troop cuts in Africa would cause alarm," *Military Time*, January 24, 2020, https://www.militarytimes.com/news/your-military/2020/01/24/why-us-troop-cuts-in-africa-would-cause-alarm/

47. Helene Cooper, "Plan to Cut U.S. Troops in West Africa Draws Criticism From Europe, January 14, 2020, https://www.nytimes.com/2020/01/14/world/africa/milley-troops-withdraw.html

Chapter 3

48. Kerry A Dolan, "The Forbes Billionaires List: Africa's Billionaires 2020," CNBC Africa, February 21, 2020, https://www.cnbcafrica.com/special-report/2020/02/21/the-forbes-billionaires-list-africas-billionaires-2020/

49. David Leonhardt, "Our Broken Economy, in One Simple Chart," *The New York Times*, August 7, 2017, https://www.nytimes.com/interactive/2017/08/07/opinion/leonhardt-income-inequality.html

50. Emily Feng, David Pilling, "The other side of Chinese investment in Africa," *Financial Times*, March 26, 2019, https://www.ft.com/content/9f5736d8-14e1-11e9-a581-4ff78404524e

51. Faras Ghani, "Black lives matter, 'even the ones drowning in the Mediterranean,'" *Al Jazeera*, July 16, 2020, https://www.aljazeera.com/indepth/features/black-lives-matter-drowning-mediterranean-200715170152666.html

52. "Land migration in Africa twice as deadly as Mediterranean, says UNHCR," *DW*, November 3, 2019, https://www.dw.com/en/land-migration-in-africa-twice-as-deadly-as-mediterranean-says-unhcr/a-51096086

53. Lorenzo Tondo, Angela Giuffrida, "Warning of 'dangerous acceleration' in attacks on immigrants in Italy," *The Guardian*, August 3, 2018, https://www.theguardian.com/global/2018/aug/03/warning-of-dangerous-acceleration-in-attacks-on-immigrants-in-italy

54. Martin Arostegui, "Spain Orders Mass Deportation of African Migrants," *VOA*, August 30, 2018, https://www.voanews.com/europe/spain-orders-mass-deportation-african-migrants

55. "Julius Malema | Full Address and Q&A | Oxford Union," Oxford Union via YouTube, January 10, 2016, https://www.youtube.com/watch?v=VZkUeZI8VtY

56. Feng, Pilling, *Financial Times*, https://www.ft.com/content/9f5736d8-14e1-11e9-a581-4ff78404524e

57. Brice R. Mbodiam, "Cameroon: Cicam plans to boost performance by introducing 15 mln face-masks in the market monthly," *Business In Cameroon*, April 13, 2020, https://www.businessincameroon.com/economy/1304-10196-cameroon-cicam-plans-to-boost-performance-by-introducing-15-mln-face-masks-in-the-market-monthly

58. Neil Munshi, "The fight for west Africa's fish," *Financial Times*, March 12, 2020, https://www.ft.com/content/0eb523ca-5d41-11ea-8033-fa40a0d65a98

59. Mona Samari, "Report: In Ghana, Chinese Trawlers Strip Fisheries Using Local Cover," *The Maritime Executive*, September 13, 2019 https://www.maritime-executive.com/features/report-in-ghana-chinese-trawlers-strip-fisheries-using-local-cover

60. Samari, *The Maritime Executive*, https://www.maritime-executive.com/features/report-in-ghana-chinese-trawlers-strip-fisheries-using-local-cover

61. Chloé Farand, "As rich countries slow walk green finance, Putin offers Africa an alternative," *Climate Home News*, October 25, 2019, https://

www.climatechangenews.com/2019/10/25/rich-countries-slow-walk
-green-finance-africa-looks-putin/

62. "First taste of chocolate in Ivory Coast - vpro Metropolis," *VPRO Metropolis* via YouTube, February 21, 2014, https://www.youtube.com/watch?v=zEN4hcZutO0

63. "5 Companies That Provide Jobs, Not Charity," *Forbes*, https://www.forbes.com/pictures/fefl45keei/madcasse/#478248796a63

64. "CBS News finds children mining cobalt in Democratic Republic of Congo," *CBS News* via YouTube, March 5, 2018, https://www.youtube.com/watch?v=OTEVHykWZqk

65. Lisa Hänel, "Why the world needs to recycle its wastewater," *DW*, March 22, 2018, https://www.dw.com/en/why-the-world-needs-to-recycle-its-wastewater/a-43078934

66. "Water For Kiunga," GivePower Foundation, August 8, 2018, https://www.youtube.com/watch?time_continue=5&v=a69712Yb3Hk

67. "Water For Kiunga," GivePower Foundation, August 8, 2018, https://www.youtube.com/watch?time_continue=5&v=a69712Yb3Hk

68. "2017 Cone Communications CSR Study," Cone (a Porter Novelli Company), https://www.conecomm.com/research-blog/2017-csr-study

Chapter 4

69. "CPI 2019 Global Highlights," *Transparency International*, referenced August 4, 2020, https://www.transparency.org/cpi2019?/news/feature/cpi-2019

70. Ben DiPietro, "FCPA Fears Hinder U.S. Companies Considering Africa," *The Wall Street Journal*, July 23, 2014, https://blogs.wsj.com/riskandcompliance/2014/07/23/fcpa-fears-hinder-u-s-companies-considering-africa/

71. Aubrey Hruby, Jake Bright, *The Next Africa*, (Thomas Dunne Books, St. Martin's Press: 2015), p.131

72. Aubrey Hruby, Jake Bright, *The Next Africa*, p.133

73. Acha Leke, Mutsa Chironga, Georges Desvaux, *Africa's Business Revolution* (Harvard Business Review Press: 2018), p.177-8

74. "Angola recovers more than $5bn in stolen assets," *Al Jazeera*, December 17, 2019, https://www.aljazeera.com/news/2019/12/angola-recovers-5bn-stolen-assets-191217172830128.html

75. "The World Bank In Rwanda," The World Bank, referenced August 4, 2020, https://www.worldbank.org/en/country/rwanda/overview

76. "Senegal's Macky Sall denies BBC's corruption report against brother," *BBC*, June 6, 2019, https://www.bbc.com/news/world-africa-48540075

77. Nick Squires, "San Marino seizes $19m from Congo dictator who spent $100,000 on crocodile shoes," *The Telegraph*, September 12, 2019, https://www.telegraph.co.uk/news/2019/09/12/san-marino-seizes-19m-congo-dictator-spent-100000-crocodile/

78. Joe Palazzolo, "From Watergate to Today, How FCPA Became So Feared," *The Wall Street Journal*, October 2, 2012, https://www.wsj.com/articles/SB10000872396390444752504578024791676151154

79. Reagan R. Demas, "Moment of Truth: American University International Law Review," *American University International Law Review*, p.367-8

80. Reagan R. Demas, *American University International Law Review*, p.335

81. Martin Gould, "Trump Slams FCPA Law, Killing American Business," *Newsmax*, May 15, 2012, https://www.newsmax.com/Newsfront/Trump-bribery-foreign-business/2012/05/15/id/439104/

82. Adam Pollock, Sarah Bayer, "Whistleblowers and the FCPA Under the Trump Administration," *Law.com: New York Law Journal*, June 12, 2019, https://www.law.com/newyorklawjournal/2019/06/12/whistleblowers-and-the-fcpa-under-the-trump-administration/?slreturn=20190901000659

83. Richard L. Cassin, "Congress votes to kill extractive industries disclosure rule," *The FCPA Blog*, February 6, 2017, https://fcpablog.com/2017/02/06/congress-votes-to-kill-extractive-industries-disclosure-rule/

84. Reagan R. Demas, *American University International Law Review*, p336-368

85. Jim Letten, Caroline B. Smith, "2019 Developments and Trends in the Federal Corrupt Practices Act (FCPA) & Global Anti-Corruption Efforts, Part 1 of 3," *JD Supra*, June 28, 2019, https://www.jdsupra.com/legalnews/2019-developments-and-trends-in-the-72835/

Chapter 5

86. Acha Leke, Mutsa Chironga, Georges Desvaux, *Africa's Business Revolution* (Harvard Business Review Press, 2018) p.xi

87. Luke Patey, "The Chinese Model is Failing Africa," *Financial Times*, August 26, 2018 https://www.ft.com/content/ca4072f6-a79f-11e8-a1b6-f368d365bf0e

88. Nirav Patel, "Figure of the week: Electricity access in Africa," *Brookings Institution*, March 29, 2019 https://www.brookings.edu/blog/africa-in-focus/2019/03/29/figure-of-the-week-electricity-access-in-africa/

89. "Samasource Founding Story", Samasource, Cited May 16, 2020 https://www.samasource.com/our-story

90. Emma Okonji, "GE Nigeria Trains 250 Entrepreneurs in Two Years, Launches Portal," *This Day*, December 10, 2018 https://www.thisdaylive.com/index.php/2018/12/10/ge-nigeria-trains-250-entrepreneurs-in-two-years-launches-portal/

91. Emily Schmall, "BET Founder Robert Johnson's Liberian Resort: An Oasis of Calm," *AOL*, February 19, 2011, https://www.aol.com/2011/02/19/bet-founder-runs-oasis-of-calm-in-liberia/

92. "A Year in Purpose: The Top 10 Trends of 2019 Pt. 1," Cone (a Porter Novelli Company), December 13, 2019, https://www.conecomm.com/insights-blog/2019/12/13/a-year-in-purpose-the-top-10-trends-of-2019-pt-1

Chapter 6

93. Yaw Dwomoh, "The African narrative: For Africans, by Africans," *Biz Community*, May 30, 2019, https://www.bizcommunity.com/Article/196/713/191326.html

94. "World Bank – IMF Guilty of Promoting Land Grabs, Increasing Inequality," *La Via Campesina*, October 8 2018, https://viacampesina.org/en/world-bank-imf-guilty-of-promoting-land-grabs-increasing-inequality/

95. Richard Behar, "World Bank Spins Out Of Control: Corruption, Dysfunction Await New President," *Forbes*, June 27, 2012, https://www.forbes.com/forbes/2012/0716/feature-world-bank-robert-zoellick-too-big-to-fail.html#5497354219dd

96. "Are Failed Infrastructure Projects Linked to the Presence of the IMF or World Bank? Read on …," *The Wharton School, University of Pennsylvania*, September 7, 2005, https://knowledge.wharton.upenn.edu/article/are-failed-infrastructure-projects-linked-to-the-presence-of-the-imf-or-world-bank-read-on/

97. Kudakwasahe Mugari, "Zimbabwe: Outrage as African Union Fires Zimbabwe-Born Envoy," *All Africa*, October 16, 2019, https://allafrica.com/stories/201910160104.html

98. Jerry John Rawlings, Twitter Post, October 13, 2019, https://twitter.com/officeofJJR/status/1183525648972816384

99. Jean-Christophe Servant, "China steps in as Zambia runs out of loan options," *The Guardian*, December 11, 2019, https://www.the-guardian.com/global-development/2019/dec/11/china-steps-in-as-zambia-runs-out-of-loan-options

100. Lou Kilzer, Andrew Conte, "Africa's wealth floods offshore as corrupt leaders, corporations use banks to hide fortunes," *Trib Live*, October 20, 2012, https://archive.triblive.com/local/pittsburgh-allegheny/africas-wealth-floods-offshore-as-corrupt-leaders-corporations-use-banks-to-hide-fortunes/

101. Robbie Gramer, Jefcoate O'Donnell, "How Washington Got on Board With Congo's Rigged Election," *Foreign Policy*, February 1, 2019, https://foreignpolicy.com/2019/02/01/how-washington-got-on-board-with-congos-rigged-election-drc-tshisekedi-kabila-great-lakes/

102. Index Mundi, Country Comparison > Oil - production > TOP 20, referenced August 5, 2020, https://www.indexmundi.com/g/r.aspx?v=88&t=20

103. Amber Pariona, "Top 10 Oil Producing Countries in Africa," *World Atlas*, October 10, 2017, https://www.worldatlas.com/articles/top-10-oil-producing-countries-in-africa.html

104. Angela Ajodo-Adebanjoko, "Towards ending conflict and insecurity in the Niger Delta region," *Accord*, January, 2017, https://www.accord.org.za/ajcr-issues/towards-ending-conflict-insecurity-niger-delta-region/

105. Justin Findlay, "Largest Ethnic Groups In Nigeria," *World Atlas*, July 18, 2019, https://www.worldatlas.com/articles/largest-ethnic-groups-in-nigeria.html

Chapter 7

106. Acha Leke, Mutsa Chironga, Georges Desvaux, Africa's Business Revolution (Harvard Business Review Press: 2018), p.5

107. Acha Leke, Mutsa Chironga, Georges Desvaux, Africa's Business Revolution (Harvard Business Review Press: 2018), p.5-6

108. Linus Unah, "In a Local Beer, a National Hero," *Eater*, November 26, 2019, https://www.eater.com/2019/11/26/20960522/hero-lager-beer-nigeria-igbos-history

109. David T. Burbach, "The Coming Peace: Africa's Declining Conflicts," *Oxford Research Group*, September 22, 2016, https://www.oxfordresearchgroup.org.uk/blog/the-coming-peace-africas-declining-conflicts

110. Omer Mbadi, "Cameroon: With Heineken's exit, Castel has sole command of SABC," *The Africa Report*, August 7, 2020, https://www.theafricareport.com/36643/cameroon-with-heinekens-exit-castel-has-sole-command-of-sabc/

111. "Guinness Cameroun is the world's fifth largest Guinness market by volume and the second largest in Africa." *Diageo.com*, referenced August 7, 2020, https://www.diageo.com/en/our-business/where-we-operate/africa/guinness-cameroun/

Chapter 8

112. Prosper Africa home page, International Trade Administration, referenced August 5, 2020, https://www.trade.gov/prosper-africa#

113. Daniel F. Runde, "Strategic Directions for the United States International Development Finance Corporation (DFC)," *Center for Strategic and International Studies*, September 24, 2019,https://www.csis.org/analysis/strategic-directions-united-states-international-development-finance-corporation-dfc

114. "U.S. International Development Finance Corporation Begins Operations," *US International Development Finance Corporation*, January 2, 2020,https://www.dfc.gov/media/press-releases/us-international-development-finance-corporation-begins-operations

115. Kaelyn Forde, "US ups investment in Africa to counter China's influence," *Al Jazeera*, June 18, 2019, https://www.aljazeera.com/ajimpact/ups-investment-africa-counter-china-influence-190618203434468.html

116. "PRIVATE SECTOR ENGAGEMENT," *USAID*, referenced August 5, 2020, https://www.usaid.gov/work-usaid/private-sector-engagement

117. "How to Become a Federal Government Contractor," USA.gov, referenced August 5, 2020, https://www.usa.gov/become-government-contractor

Chapter 9

118. "A Year in Purpose: The Top 10 Trends of 2019 Pt. 1," Cone (a Porter Novelli Company), December 13, 2019, https://www.conecomm.com/insights-blog/2019/12/13/a-year-in-purpose-the-top-10-trends-of-2019-pt-1

119. Cone, December 13, 2019, https://www.conecomm.com/insights-blog/2019/12/13/a-year-in-purpose-the-top-10-trends-of-2019-pt-1

120. Irene Yuan Sun, "Africa will take China's place as the next factory of the world," *Quartz Africa,* November 6, 2017, https://qz.com/africa/1120730/africa-will-be-the-next-factory-of-the-world/

121. Sun, *Quartz Africa,* November 6, 2017, https://qz.com/africa/1120730/africa-will-be-the-next-factory-of-the-world/

122. "A conversation with Jay Ireland, former president and CEO, GE Africa," McKinsey & Company, February 4, 2019, https://www.mckinsey.com/featured-insights/middle-east-and-africa/a-conversation-with-jay-ireland-former-president-and-ceo-ge-africa

123. Acha Leke, Mutsa Chironga, Georges Desvaux, Africa's Business Revolution (Harvard Business Review Press: 2018), p.167

124. "GE In Sub-Saharan Africa," GE.com Africa, referenced August 5, 2020, https://www.ge.com/africa/company/ge-sub-saharan-africa

125. "GE Reinforces Commitment to Improve Energy Access in West Africa," GE, April 04, 2019, https://www.genewsroom.com/press-releases/ge-reinforces-commitment-improve-energy-access-west-africa

126. "OUR WORK: MADAGASCAR," Beyond Good, referenced August 5, 2020, https://www.beyondgood.com/our-work/madagascar

127. "OUR WORK: MADAGASCAR," Beyond Good, referenced August 5, 2020, https://www.beyondgood.com/our-work/madagascar

128. Home page, GivePower.org, referenced August 5, 2020, https://givepower.org/

About the Author

Evaristus Nkongchu straddles two worlds, serving as a bridge between his African homeland and America. An immigrant from Cameroon and now a seasoned attorney and entrepreneur, he is a living example of the American Dream fulfilled, and he has a vision for a similar dream to become the reality across Sub-Saharan Africa.

Evaristus Nkongchu is the founder and managing attorney of African Legal Concierge, PLLC and founder and CEO of Alkebulan Ventures, LLC. An accomplished negotiator, litigator, and entrepreneur, he provides strategic and legal support for investment across Africa.

Also a deal maker and negotiator, Mr. Nkgonchu represents and counsels individuals and businesses on a broad range of business transactions such as mergers & acquisitions, corporate governance and compliance, due diligence on real estate transactions, contracts, purchases, and sales agreements, and NGO governance. He lives in Houston with his wife and children.

More information: AfricanLegalConcierge.com

CPSIA information can be obtained
at www.ICGtesting.com
Printed in the USA
LVHW102134270722
724601LV00010B/45/J